Larry Ricciardelli

◆ FriesenPress

One Printers Way
Altona, MB R0G 0B0
Canada

www.friesenpress.com

Copyright © 2022 by Larry Ricciardelli
First Edition — 2022

All rights reserved.

No part of this publication may be reproduced in any form, or by any means, electronic or mechanical, including photocopying, recording, or any information browsing, storage, or retrieval system, without permission in writing from FriesenPress.

ISBN
978-1-03-912955-9 (Hardcover)
978-1-03-912954-2 (Paperback)
978-1-03-912956-6 (eBook)

1. BIOGRAPHY & AUTOBIOGRAPHY, PERSONAL MEMOIRS

Distributed to the trade by The Ingram Book Company

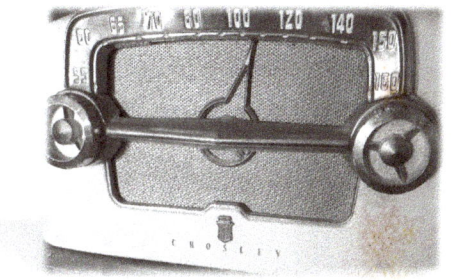

CHAPTER 1
FIRST MEETING
JUNE 1950

He sounded nice enough. Maybe too nice. And the *way* he talked was so grown up. I was only eleven, but I was curious about this boy. "Lolly and Billy," he smiled. "That has a nice ring to it. I think we'll be really good friends."

"Uh yeah, I guess we will." He was older than me for sure. Maybe even fifteen, but whatever he was, he was like no other kid I'd ever met.

Then something weird happened. All of a sudden he stopped talking and started walking. Squinting into the sunlight, he moved casually across the sidewalk towards the highway. Seemed to be in some kind of a trance, totally unaware of a puddle or the traffic!

Larry Ricciardelli

"Watch out!" A red Toronto Telegram truck slammed on the brakes just as Billy was about to step off the curb. A teenager jumped off the truck's rear platform and hurled a thick, wire-bound bundle of newspapers towards the smoke shop door.

"What are ya, stupid or somethin'?" the bundle tosser shouted as he bounced up onto the platform and whacked the side of the truck.

"Didn't you see that truck?" I walked over to Billy, who had stepped back onto the sidewalk where he stood stock-still, as rigid as the bus stop pole at the corner . He gazed out across the highway but appeared to be staring at nothing.

Five minutes earlier, I had come out of Mr. O'Brien's smoke shop with my nose buried in a *Blackhawk* comic book. *Wow! Get a load of those jet fighters.*

"You like *Blackhawk* comics?"

"Huh?" I looked up. A boy I'd never seen before had me staring at his bluer- than-blue eyes, his sharply defined facial features and his neatly parted blonde hair. He must have been fresh from the barber shop next door. There was that distinctive smell of Brylcream in the air. You could pick up it a mile away.

"Uh, yeah, I do."

"Can I look? I love those sharp-looking uniforms they wear."

"Sure. Um... you like the jet fighter planes?"

"Uh huh," he murmured, flipping a page or two. "You new in the neighbourhood?"

"A couple of months ago, we moved in. Just at the corner of McIntosh," I said, pointing down the block.

"Oh, I'm on McIntosh too. Farther along." He looked at me now in a way that made me squirm inside. Excited but hesitant all at once. "My name's Billy, by the way." He handed me back the comic.

"My name's Laurence." I felt silly saying it. "But everyone calls me Lolly."

Now I was staring at someone who had turned into a statue. *What should I do?* I mean, I couldn't just walk away from him, so I ran up to the open door of the barbershop. I'd hardly got a word out when Mr. Staley left a lathered-up customer sitting in the chair and ran outside. "Did he have another spell?" He looked into Billy's glazed-over eyes.

"I don't know. He just clammed up a minute ago."

"Stay here. Keep an eye on him. I'll go call his mom."

As Mr. Staley stepped back inside, a dark green, very expensive-looking car pulled up at the curb. Leaving the motor running, a man got out and walked over to Billy.

"In the car," he ordered. "Nothing wrong here. He's in no danger." The man gripped the boy's elbow, steered him into the front seat of the car, and drove off. I stood for a minute staring as the sleek looking car turned down Sandown. Was it an Oldsmobile? Or maybe a Cadillac, like the ones Dad talks about. Then I remembered the newspaper. My father liked to check the stock market before heading off to work. I sure didn't want to forget Dad's newspaper. I was in and out of Mr. O'Brien's store, but a lot faster this time.

"I met this boy, Mom. I've never seen him before, and something weird happened." My mother poured boiling water into a teapot and sat down. It was always hot tea at our house no matter the time of year.

"I'd like to hear all about it but a little quieter, please. Your father isn't up just yet."

"Huh?"

"He won't be leaving for the hotel today until five."

Dumping two heaping spoonfuls of sugar into my cup, I waited for Mom to pour in the milk, and the tea would follow in a minute or two.

"A boy you've never seen before? Did he tell you his name, anything about himself?"

"Well, yeah, I mean yes. His name's Billy, says he lives farther down the street. Must be somewhere near Graddi's, I think."

"Uh-huh. What was this unusual thing that happened?" Finally, Mom poured the tea.

"Well, we were just standing there talking about stuff."

"Such as?" Mom blew into her cup.

"He goes to that other school. You know, the one down past the church?" I took a good swig from my cup and reached for a chocolate bourbon cookie.

"Then I told him my name, and he said, 'Lolly and Billy. That has a nice ring to it.' Or something like that. 'I think we'll be really good friends.' But then, all of a sudden, he just freezes up. Stops talking."

"You mean he was suddenly unable to do *anything*?"

"Well, he could still move. He almost walked in front of truck!"

"Good heavens!" Mom took a small sip. "I have heard of that sort of thing happening to people. But not very often. Perhaps we can ask Dr. Logan about it one day. I do wonder, though, why he goes to the other school." She paused a moment to look up at the kitchen clock.

"But wait! There's more." I filled Mom in on the details, right up to when the man put Billy into the car. "Think we should call the cops, er… police?"

"Did he struggle at all?"

"No. It was like he was hypnotized or something."

"Did you see where the car went?"

"It went really slowly. Turned along McIntosh. That way." I pointed out the kitchen window and at the same time snatched a second yummy mummy cookie.

"Well, I wouldn't worry, dear. Highly unlikely that he's been kidnapped, if that's what you're thinking, but now I really must get back to Canon Smythe's stole. And Dad will be up in a few minutes."

"Okay. Did you see the front page of the paper?"

"Oh, dear. This *does* look serious," she said looking at the headline.

REDS CLOSE IN ON SOUTH KOREAN CAPITAL

"Who are the Reds?"

"That's too long a story for now. Now don't waste the rest of the day inside."

"Okay, just hope it doesn't start raining again." I'd go on up to the park, and see who was hanging around. Besides, I didn't like being around the house when Dad was getting ready for work.

CHAPTER 2
NEW NEIGHBOURHOOD

So, the police did not get called. Even if Mom had phoned the Township Police Department, they most likely would have said they were too busy to look into an incident like this one. After all, it was probably just a kid being picked up by his dad. The major problem the police had with kids, especially now on the brink of summer holidays, was keeping them out of the new, under construction houses that were popping up like mushrooms all over the streets of southwest Scarborough.

We had moved into our ranch style bungalow in April, one day after my eleventh birthday. Things were a little cramped at first. Mom and Dad of course got the master bedroom while my seventeen year old brother, John and I shared not only a bedroom but a bed. My two teenage sisters, Nan and Liz also shared a bedroom slightly smaller than ours. My brother and I would tell people that we'd won the larger room in a game of Monopoly.

Our house was exactly where any kid my age would want it to be. A few minutes walk or bike ride got me to pretty much anywhere I needed to be at a certain time: Midland Ave. Public School, the local Anglican Church and of course the barber shop. Also fairly close at hand were most of the places I *wanted* to be at any old time: Sandown Park with its natural ice, hockey/skating rink, Mr. O'Brien's smoke shop and a little farther along Kingston Rd. or the "highway", the appliance store with its display window of television sets! Next to Mr. O'Brien's, Christopher's Radio and TV was our most frequent stop along the route to and from school.

Larry Ricciardelli

Howdy Doody, Sagebrush Trail and even the World Series you could watch for free from outside the store. Oh yeah, and the bus stop for going to the movies or downtown was right around the corner.

CHAPTER 3
SOUTH OF THE HIGHWAY

A day or two after meeting Billy, I trekked down to the edge of the Scarborough Bluffs with Eddie Morrow and Peedy Wilson, a couple of guys from my Grade Five class. The attraction was a wrecked automobile, pushed off the cliffs by some teenagers on Saturday night, so the story went.

We stood at the grassy edge of the Bluffs, which sloped hundreds of feet down to the waters of Lake Ontario. The cliffs were jagged and roughly carved, and in most places, they were too steep even for experienced climbers. But the Bluffs did offer spots where you could get at least partway down. At one of these spots, we spotted an old black "Tin Lizzie" resting on its side, hard up against a dead tree. It was down about half the length of a hockey rink.

The car was the oldest one I had ever seen, like the ones in old gangster movies—a big black box with windows, narrow tires, and a motor compartment at the front. A leafless branch of the tree had skewered one of the rear windows, and appeared to anchor the car from hurtling down into the lake. The front passenger door was open and hanging by its lower hinge.

"Holy geez!" Eddie exclaimed. "How did they do that?"

"Musta had at least ten guys pushing," Peedy figured.

A seagull flew into view. I watched the bird swoop down, perch briefly on the car's radiator cap and then take off again. Tilting my head back as far as I could, I followed its flight up into the sun. All of a sudden, there was a cascade of blinking spots dancing around my head. A blurry vision of the climbing seagull was the last thing I saw before the lights went out.

Larry Ricciardelli

"You okay?" When I came too, Eddie's freckled nose was within a few inches of mine

"Yeah. I think so. What happened?"
"You passed out. Fainted." Peedy said, standing back a bit and looking a tad more worried than Eddie. "Luckily, you fell backwards, or you coulda gone over the edge."
"Wonder why I fainted?" I blinked a few times as I got to my feet.
"Maybe it was a-cra-phon-i-a. My mom says being up high can make your head go wonky. And your ears too. Can y' hear all right?"
"I can hear you guys okay, but I think we should go back now."

"If they catch those guys," declared Peedy, as we plodded up the Scarborough Crescent hill, "they could get ten years in the pen."
"You don't know what you're talkin' about, Wilson." Eddie laughed,
"My mom's a nurse y'know," said Peedy, chomping vigorously on a wad of Juicy Fruit gum. "So she finds stuff out that normal people don't know."
"Doesn't make you an expert on who goes to jail," Eddie stated as I turned down his offer of a liquorice black ball. I'd been thinking of asking Peedy if he knew anything about Billy, but now I thought, No, this isn't the right time. Peedy had mentioned 'normal people,' and Peedy was definitely a blabbermouth. He might even lump me in with *not* normal people because I'd passed out due to a-cra-pho-li-o or whatever it was. I'd wait 'til later to ask Eddie in private.

CHAPTER 4
PLAYING BY THE RULES

The second last day of school, as Eddie and I meandered along Midland Avenue, I quizzed him about the strange kid I'd met coming out of the smoke shop on Monday afternoon. "You mean Billy? The tall kid with the slicked-down hair?"

"Yeah, that's him."

"What about him?"

"Well, where does he live? He says he's on McIntosh."

"Two houses before you get to Peedy's."

"How come he doesn't go to Midland?"

"I think he got kicked out. Barfy gave him the slugs four times. At least, that's what Peedy says."

"You mean the principal, Mr. Barford?"

"Yup. Hardly anybody's seen him since the wintertime."

"Maybe that's why he acted so weird when I saw him."

"Weird? How?"

"Just stopped talkin', almost walked right in front of a truck. Then he froze up like he couldn't move or anything."

"Yeah, something weird happened to him one day at school before the Christmas holidays. He was in the washroom at recess, and he just conked out on the floor. Some kid ran outside and told Mr. Douglas. I think Barfy had to drive him home. Some people think he's crazy. Either that or he's been brainwashed by television."

"Huh?" I scrunched up my nose. "Whatta y'mean?"

Larry Ricciardelli

"Tell you later. Let's go see what Roamers is talkin' about."

Over at the softball diamond, little George Roamers was broadcasting news about stuff that had happened that morning. "Yeah, Robinson an' Holloway fightin' at recess!" he blared. The little guy's delivery was even more forceful than usual, given that his audience was one kid, who was at least a foot taller than George. "They start out just pushin' each other. Then Robinson gets this crazy look on his face and starts yellin' like Geronimo! He gets Holloway down on the ground and starts punchin' him like mad! Holloway finally gets up. The bum of his pants is torn, and he's cryin'. Says his dad is gonna get Robinson and kill him!"

Roamers looked over at Eddie and me. "Hey, how come you guys never saw this? Best fight of the year so far."

"We were takin' books up to the library," Eddie said, popping a black ball into his mouth.

"Yeah? Well, too bad." George carried on. "Anyhow, Holloway starts to walk away just when Barfy and Coalbag come running over. But Robinson gets in one real hard punch, and the snot comes flyin' outta Holloway's nose an' lands right on Coalbag's shoe!" Miss Coleburn (known as Coalbag because of her dark, brutish appearance) was the teacher on yard duty who assisted Mr. Barford (Barfy to pretty well everyone) in breaking up Robinson's second fight of the week.

It was generally agreed, among kids up to Grade Six, that Vince Robinson was the beetle weight champion of Midland Avenue Public School. His renowned status as a schoolyard brawler, though, carried little weight inside the principal's office. There were no exemptions from the punishment for breaking the 'frequent fisticuffs' rule, not even for 'Vee-Ro the Hee-Ro,' as he was known to the kids who lived north of the school. As for me, the youngest of four in our family, I figured the best way to get along in life was the safe way. I only made friends with good kids, like Eddie and Peedy, and steered as far away as possible from troublemakers like Vince Robinson. Thankfully, I had solid information from Peedy that Vee-Ro the Hee-Ro did not have my name on his target list. Peedy made it his business to gather "intelligence" about all kinds of stuff, such as the identity of the next kid who was likely to get a beating from Robinson or any other schoolyard tough guy. Actually, it wasn't so much that I was afraid of getting hurt. What really scared me about getting into a serious scrap on school property was the punishment. And that punishment? Kids called it 'the slugs.' Among teachers and parents, it was simply known as the strap. How bad was it? Well, it was always meted out by the principal inside the *nurse's* office, just in case you passed out or something. That was the reason given by Wilson, naturally.

"My mom has put bandages on guys' hands in lots of schools," he remarked as we sauntered down Kingston Road after school that day. "Why else would they take you in there to give you the slugs?"

Adding to the tales of crime and punishment, George Roamers blurted out for all the neighbourhood to hear, "Holy geez! A guy in my sister's Grade Eight class? The shop teacher whacked him twice on the ass with a piece of wood, and he just started bawlin'!"

"For doin' what?" Eddie dipped into his little paper bag for another black ball.

"For not helpin' sweep the floor."

Not to be outdone when it came to knowing the consequences of rule-breaking, Peedy offered the coup de grace: "If you get caught with a pea shooter now, they break it in two and make you eat a whole bag of extra hard peas. Raw!"

With these dire images tightly squeezed into my eleven-year-old brain, I was convinced that to engage the world in an unprescribed manner could be very dangerous, even fatal. Such was the story of a teenager who lost control of his dad's '48 Desoto back in the wintertime and plunged into the icy waters of Lake Whaktagon.

CHAPTER 5
THE YELLOW BRICK BUNGALOW

As much as I was a "play-it-safe kid," every so often curiosity could take me off the well-trodden path made straight by those in authority. One such trip outside the bounds of acceptable shenanigans happened when I ran into Billy again about a week into the summer holidays.

Late one afternoon, I was coming home from Mr. O'Brien's store with the newspaper when we spotted each other from opposite sides of the road.

He immediately walked across, seemingly unaware of the coat of thick, black oil that had just been sprayed over the gravel surface to keep the dust down.

"Hi there, I know you," he greeted me with a smile. "Your name's Lolly, isn't it?" I was tongue-tied. He looked older than I remembered him from our earlier encounter. I turned and looked out towards the highway before I managed to mutter, "Yeah, I saw you one day a while ago, uh... getting into a big green car."

"I don't remember getting into a car, but I do know we talked a little bit in front of the smoke shop."

"It was a really nice, dark green, expensive-looking car."

"Well, my dad has a car like that, so maybe you're right. If you saw me get in, I mean."

As curious as I was about what had happened to him, I felt awkward asking him about something that seemed so weird. I would try to keep things

Larry Ricciardelli

normal. "Aren't you afraid of getting oil all over your shoes?" I said. "I mean you just walked across the road, and..." A natural everyday question.

"Doesn't really matter. I'm getting a new pair tomorrow. We have plenty of money for shoes and clothes. My dad bought us a television set a few weeks ago. An RCA Victor with a twenty-one-inch screen."

"Wow! I've only seen a television in Christopher's store window."

"Well, maybe you can watch ours sometime. We also have the extra tall antenna, so on a clear night, we can get the Buffalo channel *and* the one from Rochester!"

"Huh?"

"Rochester. It's on the other side of the lake," he said pointing across the highway. I knew nothing about antennas, much less someplace called Rochester, but anyone with a big television set was someone I wanted to get to know. Again he looked directly at me with those ice-blue eyes, which made me think of Clark Gable from the movies, but without the moustache, of course. "Why don't you and I go exploring in one of those new houses down the street?"

I hesitated for a second, before gulping, "Uh, sure." How could I say no? Then, gathering my thoughts I asked, "Are we allowed to?"

"Sure, my dad's the builder. We can slip in when the workmen have gone home. Right after supper tonight."

I looked away. "I don't know. I mean my mom..."

"Don't tell her. And nobody else is going to find out we're in there."

"What if somebody sees us and...?"

"You worry too much. Just meet me at the back of the last house before you get to the vacant lot. It's the yellow brick one. See you at seven. Now watch this," he said as he began to skip back across the oil-slicked road. "I'm as sure-footed as a black cat." I didn't even get a chance to say okay.

I thought everything over again when I got home. *Billy seems like a nice kid, but Eddie says he might be crazy... Nah, if he was really crazy, they'd keep him locked up in the nuthouse all the time. What's so bad about freezing up so you can't talk? He didn't do anything terrible, and he was okay today. Maybe he's just different. And he's got a television set!... Wonder what brainwashed means? I'll ask John later. He'll be going into his fourth year of high school, so he must know about stuff like that.*

My favourite comic strip was *Mandrake The Magician*. No matter what, I never missed reading it, and that night was no exception. This character possessed amazing hypnotic powers. He would simply "gesture hypnotically" and make miraculous things happen, like turning some bad guy's gun into jello. My brother had explained that Mandrake used hypnosis to make people *think* these amazing things were really happening. Anyway, I decided after all that I was ready for a little adventure with this unusual boy and his piercing blue eyes. I might even get a little oil on my shoes, but what the heck, you had to take a chance now and then.

I ate supper alone that night. My two teenage sisters had already gone to the movies, and my brother had yet to come home from his summer job. As usual, Mom was busy with her church embroidery, and Dad had already gone to work just as he did every night of the week except Sunday.

"Goin' down to Peedy's for a while," I called out to Mom. I got up from the table with half of my chocolate pudding still in the bowl.

"Well, just make sure you're home before the street lights go on."

"Okay, Mom." The screen door slammed behind me as usual, but this time it sounded a little louder. I hadn't told my mother the truth.

There was still a good two and a half hours of daylight left, so I took the laneway to avoid being seen by anyone. A few houses down, I spotted Billy on top of a mound of excavated clay and rubble. Behind him was the yellow brick bungalow.

"Hi, Billy!"

"You're late."

"You didn't say any exact time… uh, did you?"

"Yes, I said seven o'clock!" He wasn't even looking at me, and he sure didn't sound very friendly.

"Sorry, I just…"

"Oh, it's okay," he suddenly changed his tune. "Just my mother talking."

"Huh? Whatta you mean?"

"It's complicated. See that little cottage over there?" He pointed to an old house on the far side of the lane. "Sometimes you can see old Mrs. Potter peeking out her back window. She phoned the police on my brother once for throwing stones at her cat."

"Your brother threw stones at a little cat?"

"Actually, he's my *half*-brother and it wasn't a *little* cat."

"You have a half-brother? What's that?"

"I'll tell you later. Now c'mon, we'll sneak in up near the front. Mrs. Potter can't see that far."

We got in through a basement window opening. Billy led the way upstairs. The floor was littered with building debris, mostly nails and bits of electrical wiring. The only inside door I could see that was hinged into place was the one for the hall closet.

"Well, here we are, in the house of adventure." Billy put on a pair of black leather gloves. "And that closet over there is where all the excitement begins."

"How come you're puttin' on gloves?"

"Ah, not just any gloves," he said pressing the tight-fitting leather around his fingers. "These are the gloves of Messmer the Gatekeeper."

"Who?"

"Just the name of a man with amazing power."

"And you need them to open the door?"

"I'm not sure 'need' is the right word, but they do add a touch of drama to the game we're going to play."

"We're playin' a game in the closet?"

"Yes, we are. And you get to stay in the closet for a while all by yourself. Sounds like fun, doesn't it?"

"I dunno if I wanna do *that.*"

"Nothing to worry about. It's really a test to see how brave you are." He pressed his fingers tighter into the black gloves. "Pass the test, and you become a member of the Mandrake Magicians' Club. The MMC!"

"Wow! Mandrake's my favourite comic. Y'mean there's a *real* Mandrake Club?"

"You bet there is. And I'm the president. So into that closet you go, and if you're brave enough to be all alone in the dark while I hold the door shut, I'll make you the vice-president."

"But you'll let me out when I want, right?"

"Sure thing. Just say, 'Messmer, O Messmer, please open the portal.'"

"Messmer? I thought it was Mandrake."
"Messmer is the gatekeeper. Remember?"
"What's a portal?"
"Another word for door."
"Oh, okay." I tried not to think about Billy's weirdness.

He really is just an ordinary kid, I reasoned. I mean, he'd *have* to be if he's president of the MMC.

So I stepped boldly into the tiny, shadowy space. Billy pushed the door shut tight. There was nothing to be afraid of, though. Not for someone who was going to become the vice-president of the MMC.

After ten minutes or so of pitch-black silence, I figured I'd shown ample bravery, so I called out the Messmer verse. No sound from the other side. Maybe he couldn't hear me. This time I shouted, "MESSMER, O MESSMER, PLEASE OPEN THE PORT!" Still no answer. "C'mon, I want out!" I pushed on the door, but it wouldn't budge. Now I screamed as loud as I could, "OPEN THE PORT!" There was only silence and darkness, and no way to escape. Tears started welling up. In desperation, I slammed my whole right side against the door. Finally, from the other side, I heard Billy's voice, but it sounded deeper and weirder than ever:

" 'Oh, why do you do this?' the prisoner moaned. 'Because you're *mine*,' the keeper intoned."

"Let me out!" My face was wet with tears and sweat. "Please, let me out!" In the darkness of my little prison, I was now sitting helplessly on the floor. "Please, please, I just wanna go home."

I heard his voice again, but this time it was higher. "Mommy will open the portal when it's time."

"Okay, okay! I meant open the PORTAL!"

Then everything changed. Billy shrieked, "Stop crying like a baby!"

WHAT?! Wait a minute. Did he just call me a cry baby? "Okay, that's it! Now open up!" I started kicking the door mercilessly with the bottom of my foot. WHAM! WHAM! The door flew open.

"Why'd you kick the door so hard? You could've broken it!" Billy was glaring at me, the gatekeeper's gloves pressed firmly against his hips.

Larry Ricciardelli

"Because you wouldn't let me out. That's why! But I'm out now. And you know what? You don't scare me, 'cause I've got a *whole* brother whose a lot older. He could take care of you *and* your half-brother. Put together!"

Billy's harsh tone dropped down a level. "I'd be in hot water with my dad if you'd broken that door. He blames me for everything!"

"Too bad! I'm goin' home!"

"Oh, but look, you're still a prisoner." He pointed to a chunk of rough lumber nailed across the front door. "Me thinks we'll be here all night."

"Well, *me* thinks I'm gettin' outta here the same way we got in." I started towards the basement stairs. Billy grabbed my arm.

"Wait a minute. You passed the test. There's nothing to worry about."

"Nothin' to worry about! We're not even supposed to be in here. I'm gettin' out now!" I yanked free and jumped two steps down to the landing.

"Hold it right there! Go home now, and you destroy the plan!"

"What plan? More stuff you're gonna scare me with?"

"You, you... little bugger. You're going to ruin everything!" He was shouting now, so loudly I was sure even that old lady could hear him.

"I don't care! I'm not staying here to get reported by old Mrs. Tinpot or whoever she is." I'd barely got one foot on the basement stairs when Billy's shouting turned into a high-pitched scream.

"Ahhh!"

I turned around to see Billy slumped back against the closet door and shielding his eyes with his arm. A gap near the upper corner of the plywood sheet covering the front window had made a funnel for the sun's rays that blazed through into the shadowy interior of the house.

"Are you okay?" I shouted, running back up the stairs.

"I don't know. I don't know," he blubbered. THUD! Billy crumpled to the floor.

"Maybe I better go get some help."

"No, don't leave me alone!" he cried, lying motionless amidst the sawdust and blobs of dried plaster. Then, opening his eyes, he took a few seconds to catch his breath. "I'll be all right in a minute."

"What's wrong with your eyes?"

"It's that light. It nearly blinds me." He slowly got to his feet. "You must think I'm crazy," he sobbed.

"Just because the light hurts your eyes? That's nothing to worry about… is it?"

"No, you don't understand. It's something that just happens when I get upset. Bright light makes it worse." Remembering the time outside the smoke shop gave me a cold shiver. Was he upset then? Maybe it was just the sunshine. And I just wanted to get the heck back outside into the sunshine, or what was left of it—away from that horrible dark little closet; away from this house that I shouldn't even be in; and away from this boy who seemed possessed of something very strange, and very frightening. As I started down the basement stairs a second time, Billy's voice stopped me.

"Look, I'm better now. It doesn't happen very often. Let's stay here a bit longer."

"Are you kidding? I'm gettin' outta here."

"You can't get back out that window. It's too high up."

"You think so?" I was down in the basement in a second where I picked up a sawed-off piece of two-by-four.

Billy ran down. "What are you going to do?"

"Just watch me." With the two-by-four leaning against the wall, I put one foot on the end of it and easily pulled myself up through the window opening. Billy scrambled out, right behind me.

Outside, he acted like nothing bad had happened. "Fun playing that game, isn't it, Mr. Vice-President?"

"No, it isn't, Mr. Weirdo President!" This time I was the one who took off down the street without waiting for him.

CHAPTER 6
RADIO FRIENDS AND REGULATIONS

I gently closed the screen door and kicked off my running shoes, then headed across the kitchen floor, towards the back hallway and to the bedroom I shared with my brother. At the dining room archway I paused, knowing it was next to impossible to avoid even a slight inquisition from my mother. She smiled as she looked up from her embroidery frame. "No oil on your shoes, I hope."

"No, but I took them off anyway."

"There's a fresh pot of tea right here on the table, and the rest of your pudding is in the fridge."

"Thanks, Mom, but I'm a little bushed. Just gonna go listen to the radio."

"Well, before you do, tell me what you did at Peedy's."

"Not much. Just fooled around."

"But no fooling around in the new houses, I hope." Mom moved her glasses from her forehead down to her nose before leaning over to pour herself a cup of tea.

"Don't think so." My usual response when steering a course between an out-and-out lie and a vague version of the truth.

"Well, you know they're looking out for that sort of thing, and I don't want you coming home in a police car." She took a sip of tea, and then, with her glasses back on her forehead, she proceeded to guide an impossibly

Larry Ricciardelli

thin piece of thread through the eye of a nearly invisible needle. My cue to move on.

I clicked the switch of the bedside table radio, located of course, on my brother's side of the bed. The little Crosley buzzed for a minute, then gave way to a jumble of static. A slight twist of the tuning dial brought clarity to an announcer's voice. I stretched out on the bed.

> The Rescue Squad brought to you by Wheat Strong—The Breakfast of Patriots.
>
> Hal, a young recruit hoping to become a permanent member of the squad, has just saved a seven-year-old boy from falling off the face of a one-hundred foot cliff, almost assuredly to his death. Hal is lying on the ground, breathing hard and groaning, while the little fellow, safe but sobbing, clings to his mother. Moments later, Sal Daily arrives on the scene. As you know, he is the Rescue Squad leader and long-time friend of the new recruit. Let's listen in:
> "I see the little lad is safe and sound, but Hal, are you okay?"
> "I think so, Sal, but my leg hurts like mad. The pain's so bad. It must be broken. Ahh!"
> "Sorry I had to send you out alone on this one, Hal, but I had to see if you were up for the job."
> "How did I do, Sal? Did I make the grade?"
> "Are you kidding? You've got my recommendation, buddy. I'm going in to see the boss as soon as we get back."
> "What about my leg? Don't think I'll be able to walk for quite a while."
> "Well, let's get you to the hospital for starters. Trust me, Hal, everything's gonna be okay. Hal and Sal, pals forever. Remember?"

I lay there for a while half listening to the show and thinking about my new friend. *Lolly and Billy, sort of like Hal and Sal. It does have a nice ring to it. We're not pals forever or anything like that yet. But I sure showed Billy I could make the grade. Yeah, I was scared at first when he locked me in the closet. But then I got mad and got myself out. He'll never try anything like that again . . . But poor guy! What about the spell he had? That was scary to watch. And Geez, he looked so helpless. Like Hal with a broken leg. Didn't want me to leave him alone. Kinda sorry now I left without even saying, "See you later," or anything . . . I can't tell Mom though. About any of this. If she knew what happened tonight, for sure she wouldn't let me be friends with him, period!*

> We'll get back to tonight's episode of Rescue Squad right after a word from our sponsor.

My mother was, to say the least, very particular about the friends I made. In her eyes, kids fell into three categories: good, bad, and unusual. Naturally, I was allowed to make friends with people in the good category. This would include kids who stayed out of trouble, were members of upstanding organizations such as Wolf Cubs or Boy Scouts, and most importantly, belonged to one of the major church denominations. Preferably Anglican. Under no circumstances however, would she allow me to make friends with category two, bad people. Scoundrels in this group might display bad behaviour and use improper language: vile words like "bum," "bugger," and "shit." They might commit petty crimes like stealing penny candy, firecrackers, and matches. And they most assuredly would lack any religious upbringing at all. Category three was reserved for unusual or "iffy" people. Such people might belong to a church *other* than Anglican, United, or Roman Catholic. They might dress differently from most people. Kids in category three might also display strange behaviour in public. Such people were not necessarily harmful to others but were often an embarrassment to themselves. Needless to say, Billy was a candidate for the "iffy" category three.

CHAPTER 7
BLACK MAGIC

A couple of days later, Mom heard from a neighbour about "a slightly strange boy" who lived down the street from us and who was spotted sneaking into one of the new houses on the block. "Could this, by any chance, be the boy you met just before school ended? The one who lives farther down the street?"

"Not sure, Mom. But it looks like rain, so I'd better go out and get the garbage can."

Later on that evening, Mom broached the topic a second time. "Laurence, before you go anywhere tonight, I want a clearer answer about this strange boy in the neighbourhood. If he is this Billy you told me about, then I would like to know. But, if you honestly don't know, then all right."

There was that word, *honestly*. If she'd said, "*Really* don't know," or "Don't *actually* know," I might well have continued to keep my new friend a secret. 'Honestly' however, was a killer word: on my honour, I swear to tell the truth, the whole truth, and nothing but the truth. And even the Bible laid down the law. Honour thy father and thy mother.

"Okay, Mom. I didn't really understand what you meant the first time, but now it's a lot clearer. Yes, Mother, that boy you heard about could be Billy." I was as truthful as could be expected under the circumstances and spoke with the utmost respect.

"Well, then," she said, apparently quite taken with my honesty. "You are to be very careful when you're with him. I do not want you getting into any serious trouble. I don't mind your seeing him, but I don't think you should be alone with him."

And so, I heeded my mother's warning to the letter. She said she didn't *think* I should be alone with him, which was not the same as saying I was not *allowed* to be alone with him. With this loophole firmly established, I spent quite a bit of guilt-free time with my new friend over the summer holidays.

Because of all the weird stuff that had happened up to now, I felt that if I devoted more time to my position as vice-president of the MMC, things might get a little more normal. My main job was recruitment, and so far I had failed miserably. With July and most of August already gone, our membership list consisted of two names: mine and Billy's. It seemed that other kids weren't as trusting of Billy as I was. When I offered George Roamers the position of second vice-president, he turned me down flat. "I'm not gettin' mixed up with Northcott. I heard he's headed for the loony bin. I'd rather hang around with Vee-ro the hee-ro than that weirdo!" The only kid to consider joining up was Billy's half-brother, Ronnie. He half considered joining us, but only if he could be treasurer. He demanded that members, including the president and vice-president, pay dues of five cents a week. When we nixed that idea, he said he didn't really care because he could get a job picking dew worms and make ten cents a can.

Undeterred by lack of popular support, we carried on. The two of us met Thursday, Friday, and Saturday every afternoon near the little garden shed at the back of St. Peter's Church. At first, I wanted to have meetings more often because with Peedy and Eddie away at their summer cottages, there wasn't a whole lot to do except cut my grandmother's lawn and work on other gardening jobs. However, Billy said that those three days were the only ones suitable for meetings. He had to be somewhere else the rest of the time, but he never told me where. "Just think of the movies," he said. "They save the best ones to show on Thursday, Friday, and Saturday. The best days of the week."

"By the way," I reminded him, "I still haven't seen your television set. When do you think I could come over?"

"Soon, maybe. But it's too nice to be inside on a day like today."

Another maybe. Another soon. Anyway I still hadn't had a chance to ask my brother what 'brainwashed' meant, so better safe than sorry.

Even though the church was right across the street from my house, there was little chance of being noticed by Mom since we sat behind the shed. This spot also gave us easy access to the leftover building materials from a nearby newly finished bungalow. There for the taking were scrap pieces of wood, strips of roofing- shingles, piles of bent or rusted nails, and for some kids, the most valued remnant of all—chunks of tar. Billy liked to chew this stuff. "Next best thing to bubble gum, and it's free!"

I tried it one day and spat it out right away. "Blech!"

Billy assured me that it wasn't that bad. "It's an acquired taste. Once you get used to it, it works wonders. I call it black magic. Maybe try it again later." As for the actual meeting that day, we talked about building our own clubhouse using the scrap materials at hand. "But," declared the president, "it must be constructed somewhere off hallowed ground." I was not quite sure what he meant by "hallowed ground," but as vice-president, I never asked questions about any of the president's edicts. I was quite content to sit in the shadow of the shed, shielded from the afternoon sun, listening to Billy talk about the amazing Mandrake.

"I like to think of our great magician as my alter ego," Billy said, gazing up at the clouds.

"Your what?"

"Alter ego, your other identity. Like Superman and Clark Kent."

"Oh, I thought you meant *altar*, like the one in a church."

Billy laughed. "How interesting. A secret religious identity." Then he lowered his voice a notch or two. "By day, a gentle priest, a loving man of God, but by night, a slave to Lucifer himself."

"Who?"

"Lucifer. You know, Satan. The so-called devil?"

"Oh, yeah, that silly lookin' guy with horns on his head." I chuckled but at the same time thought, Geez talking about this kind of stuff on the grounds of St. Peter's church? I mean, bad things could happen. I changed the subject. "So, Mandrake was really good yesterday, huh?"

"Of course, he was good, but speak of the devil, I think I might just try to sneak into this nice old church one night. You like that idea?"

"Huh? Sneak in where?"

"There." He pointed to the basement door, just to the right of the little shed. Then grabbing the padlock, he said, "See? It's loose. We could just..."

"I gotta go." I could get crucified if anyone found out I was hanging around a kid who was talking about the devil and thinking about sneaking into a church at night!

"Wait. Just try a chunk of black magic. It'll make you feel great! Like you can do anything at all. Anything you want to." Billy skipped out onto the church lawn. I was about to walk away when he grabbed me by the wrist and looked me straight in the eye. "The eyes of the master so deep and so blue / The eyes of the master will give power to you." That spell-binding chant suddenly, magically absorbed any lingering fear I still had of Billy's weirdness. He held out his hand. The tar had softened into a kind of plasticine, and in my mouth, it was like cheddar cheese. It was chewy, but had a maple flavour. In seconds, I felt myself floating. Floating, so it seemed, effortlessly up above the rooftops across the street. I saw a solitary TV antenna like the one Billy had described. I floated so close to it that with the slightest effort, I was sure I could touch it.

Back down on the grass, I sat still, looking up at the silent chimneys and dark-shingled roofs. Billy leaned over. "Your hand," he said, bringing my gaze back to him. I offered it without hesitation. We stayed hands clasped, just looking at each other. For those few moments, I was completely taken by his gaze. I wanted more than anything to become exactly like him. To let any barriers between us melt away. "Now," he said, "you can do whatever I do. You can use wonderful sounding words. You can make up clever rhymes. You can even have hypnotic power."

Overhead, a skywriting plane buzzed in big circles.

Instinctively, my head flopped backwards. High above us, an acrobatic pilot had spelled out C N E in big puffy letters. The three-letter message hung magically in the air for a short time before gradually dissolving into wisps of white smoke. Now my vision started to blur, little dancing dots appeared out of nowhere and right on cue, my stomach began to churn. It was like that day at the Bluffs all over again.

"I feel sick!"

"It's all right," Billy said, putting his hand on my shoulder. "It'll go away in a minute."

"No, I'm goin' home." On the verge of puking my guts out, I stumbled my way across the churchyard. All I wanted now was the coolness of our basement rec room, somewhere I could forget that wobbly basement door and that Lucifer devil guy. And Billy's black magic tar!

CHAPTER 8
THE BEGINNING OF THE END

The last Friday of the summer holidays was a scorcher. I spent a good part of the morning sitting high on a branch of the climbing tree near the edge of our front lawn. Dad had taken the car in for a new rad or something, so I didn't have to worry about him getting after me to sweep the sawdust off the basement floor. I was flipping through an old *Blackhawk* comic and every now and then thinking about the start of school. I would be back with Peedy and Eddie and Roamers. But no Billy with his hypnotic powers! He'd have to work his magic on kids at that other school. "Thank God for small mercies," as Graddi says. Uh oh, I spoke too soon. Out of nowhere, Mr. President came waltzing across the road wearing a long black gown. In this heat? It looked just like the one Reverend Foster wore every Sunday. If it wasn't for a Lone Ranger mask and the same trusty pair of black leather gloves, he could have passed for someone about to deliver a sermon.

"Club meeting this afternoon," he shouted.

Just then, Mom called out the kitchen window. "Lunch is ready."

"Gotta go." I jumped down from my perch.

"Don't forget now. Two o'clock sharp. I'll show you some really marvellous magical things," Billy called from the sidewalk.

"Don't know. Might have to clean up the basement."

Larry Ricciardelli

A few minutes later, I was sitting at the kitchen table devouring an egg salad sandwich and washing it down with generous gulps of Mom's homemade orange lemonade. As I stifled a burp, a picture of Billy wearing that sweaty, long black gown popped into my head. That image brought me back to our last meeting. The black magic, the dizziness, and almost barfing. The egg sandwich didn't look so delicious anymore. "Not hungry all of a sudden?" Mom poured herself a cup of tea while the younger of my two teenage sisters sat opposite me, nibbling a sandwich and flipping the pages of a movie magazine.

"Maybe I ate too much cereal this morning." I pushed back from the table.

"Well, why don't you wait for a bit?"

"Okay."

I was about to shuffle off to the basement when Liz piped up. "Was that that Billy kid outside?"

"Not sure. Might have been," I said, moving slowly away from the conversation.

"Oh, really, Laurence," Mom said. "Surely, you know whether or not it was Billy."

"Well, he was wearin' a mask, but yeah, I guess it was him." I took a wee step towards the basement stairs.

"Hold your horses. I thought it was understood that he was someone you should not be alone with."

"I know, but I wasn't exactly alone."

"That's beside the point. More importantly, it looked very much like he was wearing a church cassock."

"Is that what it's called?" I sat back down, knowing I had to give Mom my full attention on anything that had to do with the church. And this might take awhile.

"Yes, and it is a garment that should not be worn as a costume."

With an acute sense of timing, Liz came to the rescue. "That Billy kid is nutsy coo-coo, you know. His brother was in my class. Says he's really looney tunes."

"Elizabeth, we don't make fun of people with unusual habits."

"Sorry, Mom. His brother said it, not me."

"Half-brother," I added.

"No matter who said it, whatever the problem is with that boy, it's no laughing matter."

Liz immediately switched to a more important topic. "Can I get my hair cut like Doris Day?" she asked, holding up her magazine.

"When you find a part-time job, and you're earning your own money, you can have your hair done in any style you like." I seized upon this convenient diversion from church matters as my exit cue. "Remember we have an early supper tonight," Mom said.

"Okay, I feel a little better now. Can I... I mean *may* I eat my egg sandwich down in the rec room?"

"As long as you brush the sawdust off your pants when you come back up. And please, Laurence, if Billy comes around again, tell him that you have to help your grandmother in the garden." Mom was really being quite helpful since she had not yet laid down a strict no-play policy. Her non-prohibition had given me a chance to think more thoroughly about being friends with a category three boy who was growing more unusual by the day.

Our under-construction-recreation room, a project my father started shortly after we moved in, was the coolest spot in the house. I went down and sat on the dusty old chesterfield and began thinking about Billy again.

Okay, so Billy has some kind of problem with his brain... good sandwich, Mom. Yummy! He goes all stiff when he's blinded by light cuz it really hurts his eyes. What's the worst thing about that?... Could he be insane? Really nuts, like Liz says? Nah, he wouldn't be allowed outside if he was... Plus, it only happens when he gets upset. But what about that gown he had on? And the mask... Well, maybe it was some kind of Halloween costume he was trying out. Then there's the black magic tar. Didn't taste so bad the last time, and it really did make me feel great, like I was floating... But that stuff about hypnotic powers? That is kinda scary. Anyhow, Billy is definitely an "iffy" person... But that's kinda fun in a way because you never know what he's gonna do. And, oh, yeah, I'm vice-president of the MMC, but not doing a great job of getting new members. Wonder where I can find other kids to join, just so I won't have to be alone with him. I'll try Eddie when he comes back. Maybe Peedy, too... Wonder where Billy goes on the days we don't have a meeting? To get treatment for his eyes maybe?

After a great deal of hard thinking, I decided I would continue to be Billy's friend, at least for a few more days until everyone was back at school. I just wouldn't broadcast it all over the place.

CHAPTER 9
THINGS GET A LITTLE CRAZY

The blistering morning heat had dissipated, giving way to darkening skies. The sweet smell of rain was in the air. We sat on a couple of orange crates close to the basement door of the church.

"Good news," Billy said, rolling a chunk of tar in the palm of his hand. He bit off a chewable piece and offered me some.

I shook my head. "Hurts my teeth."

Billy smirked as he began to chew. "Okay. But here's the good news. They're closing the old school I went to last year."

"Coming back to Midland?" I pretended to sound a little bit hopeful.

"Looks like it. But only for part of the week."

"How come?"

"Have to be somewhere else on the other days." Backed by a distant roll of thunder, Billy went on, "Might even be away longer than that." I knew that as president, he had to keep certain things to himself, but I asked why anyway. Was it something to do with his eye problem? "Just something I can't talk about right now. So, let's do something else. Something exciting, after all, this is the MMC." Billy got up and donned the same mask he'd had on that morning and, of course, the black leather gloves. "I'm not waiting any longer," Billy said, pointing to the door.

"Waiting for what?" I asked.

"Until it gets dark. I'm going in now."

"Huh, where?"

35

"The church." He went over to the basement door, pulled a screwdriver from his back pocket, and began to unscrew the latch on the doorpost. I looked around, thinking someone might see us. The backdoor of the house right next to the churchyard opened. I looked back.

"Billy, hold it!" The screen door slammed shut. No one there.

"Are you coming in?" Billy put the four latch-screws in his pocket.

"I'll stay out here and keep a lookout." If the minister or the janitor happened along, they wouldn't punish me for just standing and watching. I hoped.

The floppy old wooden door cracked open at the top, but moved no further. "Gimme a hand!" Billy grunted as he struggled with both arms to pull the door open.

Large raindrops began to fall. I knew it was my duty to aid the president in whatever he was trying to do. If we got caught, I could always say I just went inside to get out of the heavy rain. Might even be some hail. "Okay, one-two-three… pull!" We pulled all right, enough to open the door *and* yank it right off its upper hinge! Billy laughed. "Looks like a drunk leaning on a lamp post."

A booming crash of thunder sent us both scurrying into the church basement. "Cobwebs!" Billy waved his arm over his head.

"Hey, look," in the shadowy darkness, I reached up and yanked on a beaded metal chain. A large incandescent bulb clicked on, revealing a huge furnace with pipes sticking out at all angles.

Against the wall was a near-empty wooden bin. Chunks of coal lay scattered about the floor. Above the bin was a window so blackened with coal dust that barely a glimmer of outside light shone through. A large-mouth shovel leaned up against the wall opposite the furnace. "So, what do we do now?" I was already feeling anxious about being in a place I knew was off-limits, let alone having wrecked the door just to get in.

"We go on through over there and upstairs." Billy pointed to another door. This one was more like a regular inside door, at least a foot taller than the one we'd left open and hanging by a single hinge.

"Then what?" I knew the farther we went in, the harder it would be to get back out in a hurry.

"Wait and see," Billy said, opening the second door quite easily. "But remember, we are still on hallowed ground." Why did he have to say that! Now I knew something bad was going to happen.

As we entered a larger room, I could hear hailstones bouncing off of the window panes. We would have been drowned rats if we hadn't ducked into the basement. With just enough light coming through the windows, we were able to make our way across the floor towards a staircase at the far end of the room. "Look at that," I pointed to what looked like a wolf's head sitting at the top of a pole. "Cubs or scouts?"

Billy laughed. "I bet there are a lot more interesting things upstairs."

"Hey! Where do y'think you're going?" a man yelled from back near the furnace room.

I froze at the bottom of the stairs, but Billy turned and yelled back, "Where do y'think? Up into the pews!"

"Just hold it right there! The both o' y' !" The man came walking towards us as quickly as his limping gait would allow. I stayed put, but Billy continued right on up the stairs.

The man looked older than my dad, but not quite my grandmother's age. "What are you and your smart aleck friend doin' in here anyway?" Without waiting for an answer, he started up the stairs. "You'd better stop right now, boy," he yelled up at Billy. "Otherwise, you'll get yourself into a whole bushel o' trouble."

I ventured up a safe distance behind the man. Upstairs in the church sanctuary, Billy stood in front of the altar, facing the pews. "I have come merely to lead us in prayer," he said to an imaginary throng of the faithful.

"Well, you sure coulda' fooled me." The man made his way up the aisle. "Good prayin' folks don't usually break in through the basement." I watched from the back, ready to plead for mercy if need be. Who knows? The man might phone the cops.

Through the side windows, the sky was beginning to brighten.

"A sign, a sign from above! The Lord has blessed me, a faithful servant of Mandrake, master of black magic." Billy's face shone as his voice rose with his arms outstretched. I had never seen him so jubilant. Sunlight was now flooding the chancel and the whole front portion of the church.

Larry Ricciardelli

"That's enough, son! Now you're bein' downright disrespectful." The man made his way up the chancel steps.

"Stay back!" Billy commanded. "Thou shalt do no harm to any living creature."

The man now quickened his stiff-legged walk toward Billy. Just as he grabbed Billy's outstretched arm, I ran up the aisle and cried out, "Don't upset him!" Too late. Billy fell to the floor, pulling the man down on top of him. I could see Billy's wide-open mouth, but there was no scream this time. Instead, a look of puzzlement appeared on his face before his jaw clamped shut.

"Does your mother know where you've been today?" Dr. Logan searched Billy's eyes for clues about his altar front seizure. Billy leaned forward on the edge of the chair and shook his head.

"Showed me where he lives, Doc," said the man with the limp. "No one home. So I brought him here."

"Okay, Jack. Fortunate you found him when you did. Who knows what might have happened."

"Well, the other young lad here helped me get Billy into the pickup. He didn't look badly hurt. Just couldn't walk on his own." Jack had come over to the church that afternoon to clean up around the furnace room. He told me on the way to Dr. Logan's office that he was the caretaker at St. Peter's. "Figured somebody had broken in when I saw the door hangin' there."

I stood looking at my friend who had both arms wrapped around himself. "I'm really scared," he said in a voice I scarcely recognized.

"I think you should stay here for a bit, chum," Dr. Logan advised, patting Billy's shoulder, "at least, until we can get in touch with your mom or dad." Billy nodded.

Trembling, he muttered, "Could I have a blanket?" A blanket? In this heat? I was sweating even standing close to the small fan atop Dr. Logan's desk, whirring about as fast as it could go.

"Sure, son." Dr. Logan took a blue, fairly heavy-looking blanket from a cupboard behind his desk. "Just remember, Billy," he said, "you've had this sort of thing before and gotten over it." Billy leaned back in the chair. The blanket seemed to have made him more comfortable, for the time being at least.

"What do you think's wrong with him?" Jack leaned towards the doctor's ear as he spoke.

"Not sure." Dr. Logan was still concentrating on Billy's eyes. "I'll get in touch with his mother and let you know if she wants to talk to you."

Billy remained huddled in his blanket, and appeared to have fallen asleep in the chair. How could he go sleep after what just happened, I wondered. A few minutes ago back in the church I had been scared, even worried. Now I was just puzzled.

CHAPTER 10
THAT SETTLES IT

"Well, thank you, Mr. Hastings, for bringing Laurence home. More lemonade?" Mom and Jack were sitting outside in the two big white lawn chairs. I was relegated to a spot on the grass.

"Least I could do, ma'am, with what happened to the other boy at the church. I thought your son might be, uh… worried." He lowered his voice slightly as I turned and watched an oil truck spraying the road as it rolled slowly up Sandown.

"I can assure you that you won't have any more trouble from Laurence." Mom gave me that tight-lipped, eyebrows-raised look. I nodded my compliance with a look of 'You can say that again'. A reassuring indication to Mom that I'd learned my lesson. Respect for the property of all churches, even non-Anglican ones like St. Peter's.

As Mr. Hastings honked and drove away, I could tell from the way Mom sat down again that it was time for a more intense discussion, and not just about the church, but also about Billy. And I knew Mom would do most of the discussing.

"Before your brother and sisters get home, I want your undivided attention," Mom said as I reached for the lemonade pitcher. "Not until we've finished." She gave my hand a swat and settled back in her chair. "First of all, are you feeling alright yourself? After what happened to Billy?"

"I am now. But it sure gave me the creeps watching him go like that again."

"It must have been very frightening."

"Yeah. I mean happening in a church and everything. And Mr. Hastings practically tackling Billy right in front of the altar!" I looked across the road to the hallowed grounds of St. Peter's. I wondered whether God would be mad at Billy. Maybe mad at me too!

"Well Laurence, these things do happen," Mom said leaning forward in her chair. "But often through no fault of our own. Except of course that you know you should not have been there in the first place."

"I did feel a lot better once we were in Doctor Logan's office."

"That's good," she said taking a sip of lemonade. "But still, I am concerned about the way you've been acting lately."

"You mean when I almost fainted in the church yard?"

"Well, partially, yes. But besides that, I know you have been untruthful with me a few times this last little while." Untruthful was another killer word. Mom rarely used the word lie or liar. Those were schoolyard words: "Liar, liar pants on fire," words. But untruthful had a particular sting to it. It was reserved for serious condemnation. "The most disappointing thing, Laurence, is that you spent time alone with Billy even after I told you not to."

Disappointing. Another barb. This one went directly to the heart. It brought tears to my eyes.

"I'm really sorry, Mom," I began my defence with my head down and fingers still plucking away at the few strands of grass that remained in the patch beside me.

"I know you are," she said gently. "So there will be no more going into places where you know you are not supposed to be."

"I know, Mom." I looked over at the driveway thankful at least that Dad had left for work. "It's just that Billy said..."

"It does not matter what he said. Billy is not well. You cannot let him lead you into doing things that you know are not right."

"Like pulling the church door off?" I offered.

"Yes. Now fortunately, Mr. Hastings is not going have you and Billy pay for a new set of hinges."

"That was really nice of him."

"Yes, it was. Perhaps you could offer to help him around the churchyard from time to time."

"School starts next week. When will I have time?"

"We can sort that out later. In the meantime, I want you to let Billy know that playing with him is out of the question for now."

"Okay Mom, but just so you know," I looked up with a cautious grin. "We don't *play* together. We *hang around* together."

"Fine. It's settled then." Mom finally poured me a glass of lemonade.

CHAPTER 11
LABOUR DAY

I'm out the back door and on my way down to where we're holding the final meeting of the MMC. I see Billy sitting astride a fallen log in the vacant lot, the one next to the lane that runs behind the houses on McIntosh. "Hi, Billy," I gulp in the cheeriest voice I can manage. No reply, doesn't even look at me. He's got a tight grip on this killer of a butcher knife. Without so much as a nod in my direction he starts plunging it into the log. "Whatta y' doing?" No reply. This is not the Billy I'm used to. Yeah, he's strange alright, but I've never seen him quite like this before. He's so intent on doing some damage to this log, but he's working at it very quietly. For the moment, the only sounds you can hear are the buzzing of the cicadas and the *chunk, chunk* of the blade gouging its way into the log.

"What's wrong?" I yank on the stem of a tall wildflower, and its lacy white top comes off between my fingers.

Now he looks at me. "You're just like every other friend I've ever had. And I know for a fact that your mother doesn't want us to be friends." He looks away.

"Huh? What are you talking about?"

"You know what I'm talking about... It's *your* mother. It's *my* mother. They always ruin everything!" He drives the knife in hard, then pulls his hand away fast. Blood's oozing from between his fingers.

"Geez, Billy, you're bleeding!" The lacy flower falls out of my hand.

"I don't care!" He grabs the knife with his other hand, squeezes it tight. He resumes his attack on the log, plunging the knife in deeper and deeper. I try to whistle, just so he doesn't think I'm scared.

At the far end of the lot a bunch of kids start playing baseball. These are regular kids with a bat and ball. The crack of a baseball bat pierces the mugginess of the afternoon air at the same time as a bus pulls out onto the highway. You can smell diesel fumes fifty yards away. I look up to see a kid toss his bat and run towards a chunk of concrete block. "Yer out!" someone yells.

None of this takes Billy away from his obsessive stabbing. "Something happened a couple of nights ago when my mom and I went to Anderson's Drive-In restaurant." He sits for a moment, licking blood from his fingers. I glance up at the kids playing ball. "We were sitting in the car having a chocolate soda." His voice flattens. "But then I went inside to the washroom downstairs." He stops gouging. "And that's where I heard it." He looks down again at the knife.

"Heard what?"

"The sound of words... it was, it was... inside my head!" his voice weakens, cracking slightly.

"Geez..."

"A voice in my head. I must be... must be going crazy!"

"Why? I mean... uh, what did it say?"

"It was a man's voice... it said, 'Billy, Billy, where are you?'" Tears come to his eyes. "And then... then it said, 'You are lost. You are lost. You are all alone.'"

"Hey, you guys wanna play?" a kid shouts from the far end of the lot. Billy looks up. I think, for a moment, he's going to yell back. Instead, he just stares out towards the highway as if the baseball kids are invisible.

He takes a deep breath before he continues. "My head hurt so much!" He squeezes his eyes shut. "Then everything just went black."

"You mean...?"

"Unconscious, blacked out. I don't remember anything else until I came to." He starts wiping his tears with the back of his hand. One side of his face is streaked with blood and dirt from his fingers. He's half war paint, half plain old tears.

"Well, I almost fainted too. In the church yard. Remember?"

"Almost doesn't count. You didn't have a voice inside your head... and you didn't SHIT YOUR PANTS!"

"Geez, Billy."

"Yeah, that's about all you or anybody can say. I HATE YOU!" he screams at the sky. I know he doesn't mean me. But that word, I've never heard anyone say it with such rage. Knowing that there is nothing he can do but cement the barrier between us, he looks straight at me. His sparkling eyes have gone dark. His handsome face has become a shadowy mask.

"Billy, you better get your hand bandaged. I mean..."

"What? What do you mean? Afraid of a little blood?"

He tries to work the knife free.

"No. Just tryin' to help."

He whacks the knife handle with his bloodied hand. "Help? Okay then, you can help. Just keep your mouth shut about me! The things I just told you. You tell *anyone* that I blacked out and shit my pants, I'll be coming after you!" He pauses, looks me in the eye, changes his tone. "Remember, evil lurks just around the corner." He tugs on the intractable knife once more. "Shit!" Then he gets up and walks away.

I'm gazing at the knife and thinking, You could easily kill someone with that thing. I wonder if Billy would ever try... Stop thinkin' about it! He's gone now, so get back to normal stuff.

A kind of hardness settles in. I'm shielded from things I don't want to feel like sadness and fear, but I wonder if they too, lurk just around the corner.

There's another crack of the hardball bat. A definite, solid sound. This time the ball soars high in the air and lands a few feet away from the log. "Hey, get the ball!" shouts a fat kid on the run. I hold it in my right hand for a moment. It's different from the softballs they have at school. Quite a bit smaller, a lot easier to grip. I like the feel of the tightly knit seams under my fingertips.

"C'mon, throw it!" The kid pounds his fist into his glove. I fire with everything I've got. Smack! Right on the leather. So long, Billy. Y' can't throw a ball that hard wearin' a cassock!

Larry Ricciardelli

By suppertime, after the whole thing with Billy, I had pretty much put to rest the possibility of him returning to Midland, at least for a few weeks. Mom had said as much when I told her about the crazy way he was hacking the log in the vacant lot. "Oh, dear." That was mom's usual response when you told her something unfortunate or even slightly tragic. "How badly did he cut his hand?"

"There was a lot of blood, and he didn't even care. And he blacked out on Saturday in Anderson's restaurant. Says he heard a voice in his head."

She sighed, "Oh dear." Then, with a look of genuine concern, she said, "There is something seriously wrong with that poor boy. And I do hope he can get some help in the new school year."

"Think he'll come to school tomorrow?"

"That's unlikely. Not for the first little while anyway. He'll be better off away from other children, I should think."

That piece of assurance from Mom was as close as I could get to a one hundred percent guarantee of a trouble-free start to the year. I would be playing a different game in Grade Six. It was time for hardball. Too bad about Billy, a kid with no friends, at least none that I knew of. But that wasn't my problem.

CHAPTER 12
THE MORNING SHIFT

Around eight-thirty Tuesday morning, I walked into the school yard with Eddie and Peedy. "Think loud mouth Roamers will be in our class?" Peedy wondered.

"We don't even know whose class *we'll* end up in yet," said Eddie, whose lips were already turning black. How could he eat those crappy little liquorice balls this early in the morning?

"We'll get Miss Flowers or Mrs. Goode," Peedy stated. "One's new and the other one's really old."

"Don't tell us," Eddie laughed, "your mother is friends with both of them." I chuckled, happy to be back with normal kids again and confident that there was little or no chance of Billy showing up. The big surprise however, was the huge number of kids milling around outside on the grass at the south end of the school. "Looks like the whole school's out here," Eddie said.

"So, how come we're supposed to sit out here?" I said as we wended our way to the back of the crowd.

"School's overcrowded," Peedy remarked quite casually. We staked out a spot in the grass where the janitor's lawnmower had marked the boundary between the school property and the adjacent farmer's field. "I heard my mom talking to Mrs. Barford on the phone about all the new kids coming in this year." Mrs. Wilson felt it her job, in addition to her duties as a nurse, to keep abreast of everything that went on in the neighbourhood. "In fact," Peedy surmised, scanning the assembled throng, "there must be at least two thousand kids out here."

Larry Ricciardelli

Right then, Tommy Credit and Gordie Cosgrove plunked themselves down beside us. "Piercy, you are so full of it," said Tommy, elbowing Peedy in the ribs. There was nothing that rankled Peedy Wilson more than having someone call him by his given name, Pierce David, or something close to it. And Tommy was number one on Peedy's list of ranklers.

"Don't call me that, Yankee Doodle!" Peedy shot back. In fact, Tommy *was* an American who'd moved up here from Detroit in the springtime. Other than that, I didn't know a lot about him except, like Billy, he was a year older than my two pals and me. Presumably, it was Tommy's advanced age that gave him the right to change younger kids' names around, or just call them by their last names. In my case, Ricciardelli was too long, so he called me "Rich."

Moments later, a hush settled over the crowd. All eyes turned towards a tall man standing on a small wooden platform in front of the school entrance. "I have some special instructions for you today," Principal Barford announced. "As you may have already heard, the north-end addition will not be ready to use until after Christmas."

"Which one's the north-end?" asked big Gordie Cosgrove, leaning over in Tommy's direction.

The ever-helpful Peedy Wilson pointed towards St. Clair Avenue. "Up that way," he said, "and I was really hoping we'd be in one of the new classrooms."

"Looks like you'll have to wait 'til the snow flies, Pussy," said Tommy, chewing hard on a long piece of grass.

"Shush!" came a voice from behind us. It was that of the ever present Miss Coleburn, who was policing the outer regions of the crowd.

"And since we have too many pupils and too little space," Mr. Barford continued, "you will all be coming to school in shifts."

"What's a shift?" blurted big Gordie.

"Quiet!" It was Miss Coleburn again.

"What this means," said Mr. Barford with just a glimmer of a grin, "is that each of you will be coming to school for half a regular school day, either in the morning or in the afternoon." Well, holy cow! You could have heard the cheers and shouts of laughter all the way downtown. "All right, everyone, quiet down now." Mr. Barford shuffled some papers and began to call out the list of teachers and room numbers, starting with the Grade Eights.

A few minutes later, when Miss Bernie's name was announced as the teacher for Grade Seven, Cosgrove grunted, "My brother says she's tougher 'n a sack o' rusty nails."

"I heard that farm boy," snapped Miss Coleburn. She then cuffed him smartly behind the ear before hurrying off to comfort some Grade Seven girl who'd burst into tears at the mere mention of Miss Bernie's name.

Peedy looked up expectantly as Mr. Barford finally came to our grade. "Grade Six, Mrs. Goode. Room four."

"Oh boy," shouted Peedy when our names were called for Mrs. Goode's class. "She's old as the hills but really nice. Just like a grandmother!" The moment Mr. Barford finished reading the list for our class, we jumped up and joined the horde heading for the south end doors.

"Can't wait!" Peedy grinned as we ploughed through the crowd at the entrance to room four. The moment we got inside the room, George Roamers broke from the pack and pounced on the last available seat. "I'm small, and quick as a rabbit. Slippery as a bar o' soap," he boasted. This left Eddie, Peedy, and me, along with about ten or twelve other kids, in the standing room section in front of the windows where we waited for our teacher to make her entrance.

When Mrs. Goode, known to some as 'Granny,' finally arrived, she stood at the doorway with one arm curled around a stack of papers and holding a cane in her right hand. "Anyone who thinks of himself as a bar of soap," she said, "may find himself on the downward side of a very slippery slope." How could she have heard George from out in that noisy hallway? I wondered. The room quickly became as quiet as a pin factory as she slowly made her way up to the front. Her shadowy grey hair was piled in a loose bun on top of her head and was held in place rather precariously by a single amber-coloured comb. At the front of the room, she neither stood nor sat behind her desk but eased herself carefully into a burgundy armchair positioned squarely beneath the King's portrait, which hung at the centre of the wall.

"I wondered why that chair was there," Eddie mouthed in his patented noiseless whisper.

"I was about to explain that," said Mrs. Goode. "I am blessed with acute hearing, which means that no sound in this room will go undetected."

Larry Ricciardelli

Eddie and I silently exchanged raised eyebrows while Peedy sighed, "Grandma."

"Yes, I am in fact a grandmother," she said looking straight at Peedy, "and that is why I am accustomed to sitting in this lovely, comfortable chair from time to time." She spoke amazingly clearly for someone of advanced years, I thought. "And while we are on the subject of sitting," she continued, "I would like some of the gentlemen who have already taken desks to give them up to the six young ladies who are yet to be seated." Surprisingly, Vince Robinson was among the first to surrender his seat.

"Young man," said Mrs. Goode, turning in our direction but making eye contact with no one, "would you mind opening the window, please?" It wasn't until she peered over the top of her glasses that I realized she was targeting me.

Without a word, I dutifully turned and reached for the window handles above the big iron radiator. Although the overall frame was quite tall, extending almost to the ceiling, the lower half of the window glided easily upward with a slight shove. Then I let out a sudden, but barely audible gasp—"Holy geez, it's him!" Billy was getting out of his dad's car in front of the school. Our eyes met as he looked up. He stared at me for a moment without expression.

"Is there something the matter?" Mrs. Goode asked. "I may have heard you say 'golly gee.'"

"Yes, I mean, no, Mrs. Goode."

"Then please, may we have your attention."

As I stood in front of the big window, still shaken by Billy's unexpected arrival, troubling thoughts entered my mind. *What if they make him do Grade Six all over again because he's gone so weird? He might end up in our class! Mom seemed so sure he wouldn't be back . . . What if he finds out that I told Mom about the knife, the blood and stuff?*

I almost didn't hear Mrs. Goode when she called out my name for the morning shift, but she said it so beautifully, just the way Dad's friend, Silvio Casimeri says it: "*Reech-ar-**dell**-ee*". Darlene Connors snickered a bit, then sat up straight when Mrs. Goode gave her a stare. Our grandmotherly teacher did not miss a thing! I was able to put Billy away, at least for the time being.

Having assigned everyone to an afternoon or morning shift, and grimacing slightly, she rose slowly from the burgundy chair. "Take good care of your knees, children," she said, still gripping her cane. "I injured mine years ago at the 1936 Olympic Games."

"Did you run in the marathon, Mrs. Goode?" Betsy Trotter piped up from her front row seat.

"Oh no my dear, nothing quite so exciting," she chuckled. "I was in a hurry to leave a Berlin coffee house, and I fell down the stairs!"

On the way home, Eddie and Peedy kept up the chatter about the benefits of being on the morning shift.

"We get our work done before lunch," said Eddie, whose dad was a milkman and delivered house to house early in the morning. "Then we've got all afternoon to do whatever we want."

"Yeah," Peedy agreed. "I like doing reading and stuff in the morning. Even if it means we have to start at quarter after eight."

As we passed Christopher's Radio near the corner of Midland and Kingston Road, Eddie spotted a single television set in the display window among several radios of various sizes. "Hey look guys, one of those new big TV sets."

We stood for a minute or so, gazing at a picture of a Mohawk headdress and waiting for something to happen. "No shows on yet," Eddie said. "It's only eleven-thirty."

"Test pattern," remarked the ever knowledgeable Peedy. "It tells y' stuff about the station."

"It's a channel, not a station," Eddie pointed out. Sure enough, across the top of the screen were the letters WBEN TV and below that, CHANNEL 4, BUFFALO N.Y. My mind drifted back to the summertime. The more I stared at the test pattern, the more I thought about Billy and the television that I never got to see. The big set in the window must be about as big as Billy's, I figured. Then I pictured him standing outside the school this morning. I thought of him the way he was yesterday out in the vacant lot. I saw him with blood dripping from his fingers and I imagined him blacking out in the restaurant. "Don't ever tell anyone what happened in the restaurant," he'd warned me. His voice sounded even louder now in my head than it had yesterday. I *did* tell Mom almost everything. Did she count as anyone? I was worried.

Larry Ricciardelli

At supper that night, I said nothing to anyone about school or anything else. Surprisingly, nobody seemed to think anything was wrong with my being so quiet. But Liz, who had just spent her very first day at high school, was doing a pretty good job of kitchen table chattering all by herself. "Patsy and I are both in 9C. So is Dianne Freeman, the Reverend's daughter. She's really nice. Has a boyfriend too, but I don't think her parents know about him. And oh yes, our homeroom teacher, Mr. Babcock? He has these really dreamy baby blue eyes. Just like Farley Granger." She closed her eyes with a sigh as she pushed back from the table.

My brother laughed, "Farley, schmarley. I had Babcock for Geometry last year in eleven. That guy's so square, even the bags under his eyes have right angles."

"Really John, Laurence is still at an impressionable age," Mom quickly cut in.

"Sorry, Mom. Stan made that one up. I just couldn't resist." As impressionable as I may have been, the suppertime banter wasn't making much of a dent in me that night. I was so concerned about seeing Billy this morning that all I could do was choke down a tiny morsel of cold chicken and half a spoonful of potato salad. John conveniently scavenged the rest of my chicken while Mom was filling the tea kettle. By the time dessert came around, my usually voracious appetite had dwindled to that of a baby bobolink. I just sat there, clutching my spoon and staring at a bowl of bread pudding. Who knows how long I would have remained in a trance if it hadn't been for Nan, my older sister. "Qu-est ce qu' il y a, mon petit?" she purred in flawless French. Even though I didn't understand anywhere near half of what she said, the mere sound of the words always seemed to comfort me.

"Uhmm?" I looked up, awaiting translation.

"What's the matter, Lolly?"

"I saw Billy today," I mumbled, looking down at my bowl of day-old bread, softened with milk and sprinkled with sugar and raisins. Desserts were not Mom's specialty.

"N' as pas peur," my sister soothed. Then switching effortlessly to English, she added. "Mom told us he's just an unusual boy, but he really is quite harmless."

Geez, I wondered just how much Mom had blabbed. Then I looked at her, sipping her tea. No, I concluded she wouldn't have spilled all the beans. But I liked the words "quite harmless" coming from Nan.

"Your sister's right, Laurence," said Mom. "Billy obviously has some problems of his own, but there's nothing for you to worry about. In fact, I wouldn't be the least bit surprised if he were sent to another school altogether. Sometimes just a change in surroundings can be helpful for someone like that."

Now that made perfect sense. Maybe a school closer to wherever he went during the first three days of the week. "That must be why his dad brought him to school today," I suggested. "They had to talk to Mr. Barford about going to a different school!" Buoyed by the assurances of my mother and her bilingual assistant, I scooped up a generous spoonful of bread pudding. "You know what, Mom? I think this delicious pudding would taste even better with jello mixed in!"

Liz then dug into her bread pudding, and as if inspired by the energy-packed dessert, she declared, "If that whacko kid bothers you Lolly, just let me know!"

"Allons enfants de la patrie!" Nan sang out. I didn't have a clue what it meant, but it sure sounded encouraging.

"Yeah, don't worry, Lol," John chipped in. "As the adding machine once said, 'You can count on me!'"

Listening to *The Lone Ranger* in bed that night, I did some counting of my own. My blessings were many. I had a mother who always listened to my problems, even if she did get after me for picking my nose and biting my fingernails. I had a big brother who was the funniest guy I knew, even if he did sometimes keep me awake playing the piano late at night. And I had two older sisters who would stick up for me anytime, even if they did hog the phone almost every night.

After the final "Hi-yo, Silver! Awaaay!" I decided to call it a night. Instead of staying awake for *Blondie and Dagwood*, I would spend a little extra time on my prayers. After giving thanks for all the good things I had, I tossed out a suggestion sprinkled with a few sugary words I'd picked up from the

Larry Ricciardelli

Reverend Mr. Freeman that were sure to be pleasing to the ear of the Lord. "Although Billy will most likely be going to a different school, if perchance, he does come back to our school, I as one of thine unworthy and humble servants, suggest that the afternoon shift would be best, Lord. That way he could get more sleep in the morning, which would be much better both for his mortal body and his everlasting soul." A nicely worded petition and for the betterment of someone I wasn't too crazy about. Talk about love thy neighbour! With that, I went to sleep right away. After all I had to be awake in time for the early morning shift.

Thanks be to the God of Abraham and Jacob and the rest, the Lord saw the wisdom of at least part of my suggestion. It turned out that Billy was indeed returning to Midland, but in accordance with my prayer, he had been assigned to the afternoon shift. That meant that he'd be getting to school around 12:30 just as we 'early risers' were on our way home for the day. Plus, Thursday and Friday were the only days he'd be there at all. I trusted that the Lord would eventually send Billy to another school, even if it took Him a while longer to figure out the right one. God, in His infinite wisdom, did not always act swiftly in situations like this.

CHAPTER 13
POLICE INVESTIGATION

It all began one October morning when I was on my to the dentist. Mom had written me a note to get me out of school early. When I handed the note to Mrs. Goode, she looked up from her arm chair, and grasping my wrist she spoke, as usual, to the entire class. "Good luck, my boy. You have nothing to fear. But remember the saying of the ancient Romans: 'Medicus dentium a pervenientibus tarde iratus est.' In other words, it's not good to be late for the dentist. So off you go now!"

On my way down to the bus stop, I spotted Billy walking up Midland Avenue. My brain was immediately abuzz with questions and dire predictions. He's on the afternoon shift, and it's only ten o'clock. Why isn't he coming to school as usual at 12:30? ... Does he know that I blabbed to Mom? Oh geez! What if he's got that knife inside his jacket?

I thought about crossing to the other side, but Billy would still be between me and the bus stop, so I took a breath and kept on walking straight ahead. If he tried anything, I would just have to make a run for it.

"You're out early," he said casually.

"Yeah, I'm goin' to the dentist. Gotta catch the bus," I pointed down towards Kingston Road.

"Well, I've got something to tell you." He looked around as if there might be somebody listening. Just then a truck pulled up right beside us. A brown uniformed delivery man got out and quickly began loading his wicker basket with loaves of bread, and other baked goods from the back of the van, which bore the familiar Brown's Bread script logo across its side panels. I felt a little safer now with an adult close by.

"How y' doin' fellas?"

"Fine, thank you, sir."

"Outta school early today, huh?"

"Yes, I'm on my way to the dentist," I said cheerily in case I needed his help. Billy just smiled as the bread man walked briskly past us and up to a customer's house. Then leaning forward just a bit, in a loud whisper he said, "Some little devil tried to burn down your garage."

"Whaddaya mean?" I looked right at him.

"Really. Your garage. There's a big burn mark on the inside wall beside the door."

"A what?"

"A burn mark. Big one. Just inside the door."

"No kidding. I better go tell my dad!" I shot off down the street before Billy could say another word. The Brown's Bread guy beeped as he passed me at the corner of Midland and Park. Down McIntosh I ran with old man Froder's dog barking at my heels. Up the driveway and into the unlocked garage. Geez, he wasn't kidding! Just to the left of the door was a large cardboard box pushed right up against the wall that was full of scrunched-up newspapers, singed around the edges. Definitely looked like it was used to start a fire. Above the box, the surface of the wood siding was badly charred.

"Mom!" I burst into the house. "Somebody tried to burn down the garage! Come and look." Dad must have heard me because he came running down the back hallway from the far end of the house.

"Good heavens!" Mom exclaimed as the three of us stood looking at the crime scene. "Who would do such a thing?"

"I dunno, Mom. Billy just told me there was a burn mark on the wall, so I came in and looked."

Dad gave the box a good kick. "Son-a ma bitch! He's-a gonna pay for!" For a moment, I thought he was talking about me. My father's thick Italian accent often left me unsure of who or what he was talking about. It scared me whenever he got upset about pretty well anything.

"Now Arthur," Mom calmly cut in, "we don't know for certain that it was Billy who did this."

"Who d'hell is gonna do this? Goddamn kid, he's-a nuts!" That was the first indication I had that Dad knew anything about Billy. What I couldn't understand was why Billy would tell me about the burn mark if he was the one who had tried to set the fire in the first place.

Mom called the police at Dad's insistence. Even though there wasn't a lot of damage, he still wanted to know for sure who tried to burn down the garage. After all, he'd stopped work on the rec room and spent the entire summer building the garage by himself with a little help from John on the weekends. "Someone will be here shortly," she said, pressing down the phone's disconnect button and then dialling a second number. "I'll have to call Dr. Toynbee and cancel your appointment, Laurence. I'm sure the police will want to ask you some questions." What a lucky break! No dentist, and I get to talk to the cops and help them solve a crime.

Shortly after lunch a black Ford four-door sedan pulled into the driveway. Two detectives wearing tweed jackets and fedoras got out and looked around as if they were surveying the neighbourhood. "They're here, Mom," I shouted from the doorway.

"I can hear you perfectly well without your shouting, Laurence," said Mom. Dad made the trek up from the basement, muttering to himself in Italian.

Outside at the crime scene, I looked at the taller of the two men. I wondered if the bulge below the lapel of his jacket was a shoulder-holster. This cop got right down to business. He bent down for a close look at the charred circle on the garage wall, surprisingly without the aid of a detective's magnifying glass. "This box," he said, kicking a large cardboard carton on the dirt floor. "Is it your garbage?"

"No, sir. We never keep our garbage in the garage," I offered without hesitation. Co-operative and informative testimony, maybe he'd let us have a look at his gun.

Meanwhile, Dad was gesturing dramatically as he spoke to the shorter man who was writing in a small notebook but saying very little. At one point, he knocked the detective's pad and pen out of his hand but kept right on waving his arms and talking.

"I'm-a tell-a you, this boy... he's *tutto pazzo!*"

"And which boy would that be?" asked the tall, gun-toting officer as he picked a singed scrap of paper out of the box.

"I think my dad means Billy, sir. Billy Northcott"

He then reached inside his jacket for what I was sure would be his gun. Instead, he pulled out a black book. "And where might we find Billy now?" he asked as he began to thumb the pages of his book.

"Probably in school, sir. Miss Bernie's class. On the second floor. Oh, and he might be wearing a pair of black leather gloves." Perhaps this piece of useful information would make me a junior detective, and I'd be allowed to watch him load his snub-nosed revolver. But no, apparently they would do that in the car or in the boiler room at the school.

"Let's go and have a little visit with the young man in Miss Bernie's class, Fred," said the taller man. Tipping his hat to Mom, he added, "I think we'll have your culprit shortly, ma'am."

We found out later that afternoon that Billy was indeed the failed arsonist. I pictured the tall detective taking Billy into the boiler room where he would finally pull out his gun. Then he'd say something like, "Okay, y' little punk, admit it. Now hand over that box of matches in your pocket."

Just before suppertime Mom called Mrs. Northcott. "Poor woman, she must be very upset about this," she said as she dialled the four-digit number. "Mrs. Northcott? This is May Ricciardelli calling… Yes, I'm Laurence's mother… No, Mr. Ricciardelli has already left for work… Yes, Mrs. Northcott, I can understand how you must feel. Certainly, if Laurence ever did anything like that… (a long pause)… But surely you realize that the police said… Well, I am sorry you feel that way. . . Of course, I'll keep that in mind. Goodbye."

"What did she say?" Liz asked, looking up from the latest edition of *Modern Screen*.

"I'm quite surprised." Mom placed the telephone receiver gently back on its cradle. "She thinks Billy had nothing to do with it at all."

"But the police went to get him out of school," I protested.

"Yes, of course they did, but Mrs. Northcott says that it's all a pack of lies."

"How could she say that?"

"I really don't understand it." Mom sat down and poured a cup of tea.

And I certainly didn't understand it either, more so because of what I heard a few days later. The word from Gordie Cosgrove, also in Miss Bernie's afternoon class, was that Billy's mother whipped him so hard with the cord of her electric iron that he was away from school for a week. But why would she have whipped him, I wondered. Unless she thought Billy had done it.

"Serves him right," Gordie said, "he must be crazy, tryin' to burn down a garage as big as yours."

"Yeah, he's really gone mental," added Tommy. "They should put that guy away in Sing-Sing." Well, that didn't happen although I wished it had. No, Billy remained in the neighbourhood for the next little while, anyway. I saw him being dropped off at school a few times, but he said nothing to me about the fire or the police. Or anything at all, for that matter.

A few weeks later on a blustery mid-November evening around suppertime, Billy caught me by surprise as I was coming out of Mr. O'Brien's. He stepped out from the shadows of the alleyway between the smoke shop and Mr. Staley's barbershop.

"Listen," he snarled, looking me in the face, "you told on me and got me into trouble with the police."

"No, I didn't. Honest!" I was ready to whack him with a rolled-up copy of *The Toronto Telegram* if he tried anything.

"Don't lie to me!" he barked as the first flakes of an early snowfall began to swirl around us. "My mother whipped the daylights out of me all because of you and your big mouth! And what's more, if you keep on going around telling everybody I'm crazy, I might just *do* something crazy. To you!"

"No! I never said anything..."

But before I could finish, and without so much as laying a finger on me, Billy turned away. And then as always he just took off. This time he ran out into Kingston Road only ten yards or so in front of a big Dominion Coal truck. The driver blasted his horn as Billy stopped in the middle of the highway for a second before dashing safely to the other side. That was the last I saw of Billy Northcott for quite some time.

CHAPTER 14
HE SHOOTS, HE SCORES!

As to Billy's whereabouts, the only details we got came from Peedy Wilson. "My mom says they sent him to the hospital in Mimico," he informed Eddie and me a few weeks later as we made our way home from school through several inches of newly-fallen snow.

"Where the heck's Mimico?" Eddie wanted to know.

"About a hundred miles from here. It's where they send people who've gone crazy or even insane," explained Peedy. A hundred miles sounded like a good safe distance, but something bothered me about this news coming as it did just before the season of 'comfort and joy.'

"I wonder what it's like, I mean, bein' in a hospital so far away from home over the Christmas holidays." I looked over at a pile of Christmas trees stacked up in St. Peter's churchyard. A sign on the church wall read: 188th SCOUT TROOP—XMAS TREES $1.75

"You feelin' sorry for Billy or something?" Eddie asked as a big snowplough rumbled up behind us.

"Yeah, I guess I am, sort of." I picked a loose stone out of the road-side snowbank.

"He'll probably come home for a coupla days at Christmas," said Peedy, "if he hasn't gone too whacky." He and Eddie got a big laugh out of that, but any kid stuck in a hospital during the holidays, I just didn't think was funny. I fired the stone at the big yellow snowplough. It bounced off one of its gigantic rear tires and landed somewhere among the Boy Scout Xmas trees.

Larry Ricciardelli

Over the Christmas holidays, I was able to put Billy pretty much out of my mind. If he did come home from the hospital, he must have stayed inside because he was nowhere to be seen. Nor did I spot him anywhere near the outdoor rink where I played hockey almost every day on my first ever new pair of skates.

One day, brutally cold winds and ice-cracking temperatures kept my pals and me inside, so Eddie and I along with Tommy, the American kid, decided to keep warm by taking in a mid-week matinee at the new Birchcliff Theatre. *Abbott and Costello Meet Frankenstein* was the movie that got three hundred or so kids to plunk down their fifteen cent-admission that frigid afternoon. The other half of the bill was a really old western that nobody cared about. Nevertheless, that one came on first.

By the time the rough and tumble cowboy asked the sheriff's daughter to marry him, happily signalling the end of the movie, the whole place was in an uproar. Kids were running up and down the aisles, tossing popcorn boxes all over the place, spitting water at one another. It got so bad that the manager threatened to stop the show altogether. From the front of the auditorium, under the house lights, he bellowed out, "Keep this up, and everyone goes home early. Now sit down and keep your little traps shut or no Frankenstein!"

Well everyone did shut up when we finally got into the first few minutes of the featured film. In fact there was absolute silence during the opening scene which was so scary that no one dared utter a sound.

A man looks out his window as a full moon emerges from behind the clouds on a drizzly night in London. His face is fearful and grim. He collapses into a chair as the creepy organ music builds. Then a close up of his hands takes our breath away. They're turning into the hairy claws of some beast-like creature right before our eyes! But his face is undergoing an even more frightening transformation. In addition to a massive profusion of hair growing over his cheeks and chin, two enormous canine teeth protrude upward from his lower jaw. Now jerking his head from side to side and snarling like a vicious dog, the man-beast tears at his clothes and then begins to rip the chair apart. In minutes he's wrecked the entire room. The scene mercifully comes to an end as daylight appears through the window and the sky begins to clear. With the arrival of dawn the man, now lying on the floor, gradually resumes his normal appearance.

With characters like the Wolfman, Frankenstein, and Count Dracula, the movie packed plenty of excitement and suspense around the comedy antics of Abbott and Costello. In the big climax the Frankenstein monster is doused in gasoline and set ablaze as he lumbers stiff legged right off the end of a pier. As great as that ending was, what stuck in my imagination was the scene at the beginning where the man turns into a raging monster. And adding a touch of personal eeriness to the scene was the character's name—Laurence Talbot. "See the way the Wolfman went nuts and wrecked his whole room?" Tommy remarked as we rode home on the bus.

"Yeah, and all because of the full moon," added Eddie.

"That wasn't the only reason," countered Tommy. "The guy was already mentally derailed."

Geez, it made me really uncomfortable whenever I heard about anyone who was "mental" anything. Even the sound of the word made me cringe. I sat quietly between my two friends, the three of us taking up most of the long seat at the very back of the bus. Neither Eddie nor Tommy seemed to remember the name Laurence Talbot, but it spun around in my head like a broken record.

Instead of going right home, I walked up the street to my grandmother's house. Normally, my regular Wednesday visit to Graddi's would have been later on in the evening when Uncle George was home. With Mom out at an Altar Guild meeting, though, I didn't want to get stuck at home alone with Dad while he was getting ready for work. He could get mad at me for almost anything.

"Well, how was the picture show?" Graddi asked, pouring boiling water into the teapot.

"Pretty good, except for the part with the Wolfman." I plunked down on a kitchen chair.

"The Wolfman?"

"Yeah, it kinda scared me."

"Well, let's have some biscuits and tea while you tell me all about it." Although I didn't exactly feel like going into details about that frightening opening scene, once I started to munch on a couple of fresh-from-the-oven tea biscuits, I was able to tell my grandmother about the whole movie.

"That does sound rather upsetting," Graddi remarked as she got up from the table to start making Uncle George's supper. "When I was your age and heard a frightening story or saw a play that upset me, I would often try to find a good book to read. Quite often, a story about a famous person."

"I heard a story on the radio once about Alexander Graham Bell. Did you ever hear stories like that on the radio?"

"Oh no," she laughed, "we didn't have the radio when I growing up in England. The very first wireless broadcast I ever heard was much later on. But there were always books to read. Let me look and see if I still have something that you might like."

In bed that night, I started a book Graddi had found in Uncle George's bookcase. It was the story of a boy growing up in the slums of Manchester who eventually becomes a Member of Parliament. I struggled through the first couple of pages, hoping to purge my imagination of uncontrollable people like the Wolfman—him of course, and Billy, who was now in a hospital for people who'd gone mental. Unfortunately, there were just too many words I didn't understand, so the book wasn't much help in ridding my mind of images of crazed monsters and weird kids. I mean, the thought of a man, a guy with my own name, turning into a monstrous animal, even in a made-up movie story was the stuff of nightmares.

So, I put the book aside, said a silent thank you to my grandmother, and then reached for the radio on John's night table. I switched on the little Crosley and waited. Through the bedroom window, I looked out at a starless winter sky wondering if a full moon was hiding behind the clouds. Seconds later, the radio came to life.

"Hello Canada, and hockey fans in the United States." I'd heard that voice a few times before, and that night it came as a much-needed distraction.

The little I knew about professional hockey came from my brother, who would sometimes listen to games when I was half asleep. Pro hockey was clean and fast. That much I got from the newspaper photos John collected. In hockey, there was no room for weird kids or monsters. As I listened to the radio voice, the name Laurence Talbot and those fretful words like "mental" and "insane" gradually faded from my mind.

"Less than five minutes to go in the period." The voice was high-pitched, strident at times, but for me it was as comforting as a warm woolen blanket.

> "The Leafs are with a man advantage now as Bentley dipsy-doodles up to the Detroit line. Now he stickhandles in, moves to the left of Kelly… and here's Meeker streaking in on the right-wing! Pass… right in front. Shot! Oh, and a great save by young Sawchuck! Puck in the corner, dug out by Watson, who takes a hard hit from Pavelich but gets it back to Barilko. Barilko waits… moves away from the boards, gets around Reise… moves in… he shoots. Rebound right to Bentley… HE SCORES!"

Above the thunderous roar of the crowd, the radio voice rang out.

> "So the Maple Leafs go ahead 1-0 on Max Bentley's ninth goal of the season assisted by young Bill Barilko. But it was Bentley with his patented stick work who started the play, and eventually beat Terry Sawchuck, who'd already made two sparkling saves with Gordie Howe sitting out a two-minute penalty for elbowing."

I closed my eyes and pictured the scene downtown at Maple Leaf Gardens. I vaguely recalled going there with John and Uncle Dick when I was about four years old. That distant memory was now brightened by the radio voice, which gradually sent me off into a snuggly winter slumber. I could see Teeder Kennedy and Sid Smith racing in on goal, Bill Barilko and Jim Thomson breaking up a play by Detroit's 'Production Line' of Abel, Lindsay, and Howe, and picture Max Bentley stickhandling his way to a second goal. These wonderful images took me to a place far away from the monstrous Wolfman and from poor Billy's blood stained knife.

CHAPTER 15
WINTERTIME BULLIES

January meant back to school; however, the days of 'mornings or afternoons only' had come to an end. The new addition was finally open and ready to be occupied by happy little six and seven-year olds.

"Well, same old classroom, same old desk," Eddie grumbled, "and we're in there from nine to three-thirty."

"Yeah, but at least we get to have recess," I reminded my pals as we exited through the doors at the south end of the school. Since the shift system had allowed us only a five-minute indoor break, it was great to be outside again at ten-thirty in the morning.

The first school day of 1951 was unusually mild at five degrees above freezing, even though by recess time the early morning sunshine was beginning to disappear. For the moment however, it was still the kind of day that, when bundled up in your winter duds, you could work up a sweat doing just about anything. After we got tired of kicking an old tennis ball around on a bare patch of pavement, I yelled out, "Okay you guys, time out for a snack. Anybody want a mince pie?" I opened a crumpled paper bag that contained the last of the Christmas treats my grandmother had made. We tucked into these tasty little pastries as we walked up to take a look at the new, north-end addition.

"Hey, kid," someone barked. "How about sharin' the wealth, eh?" Walking towards us were two older kids we'd never seen before, but they looked like definite tough guys, probably in Grade Seven or Eight.

With the yard duty-teacher nowhere in sight, I answered cautiously, "None left. Sorry."

"Well, next time y' better have some goodies for me and my buddy." One of the tough guys then looked each of us in the eye and added, "We're gonna remember you little punks." Just then, Mr. Mistletoe, the shop teacher came into view wearing a scowl so menacing that the ruffians immediately stuffed their hands into their coat pockets and shuffled away.

"I'll bet those two guys don't even go to our school," Peedy said as Mr. Mistletoe checked his wristwatch.

"How do you know?" Eddie shivered a little with the sun now completely hidden behind a bank of clouds.

"Just got a feeling."

"Well, I've got a feeling it's gonna snow pretty soon," I said

as Mr. Mistletoe unleashed three ear-splitting clangs of the school bell.

As it turned out, Peedy and I were both right about our feelings. That night and all the next day, snow fell 'by the friggin' truckload,' as our school janitor, Mr. Hopkins, put it. Before and after school, we'd see him shovelling and cursing as he tried to clear the snow from around the entranceways.

By Thursday, we were living in a winter wonderland. "This is the closest thing to a blizzard I've ever seen, and my mom grew up in Norway," Eddie exclaimed as we made our way home that afternoon. I didn't quite get the connection between Eddie's mom being from Norway and the huge snowstorm we were actually trudging through, but then that was Eddie.

"Yeah. Hey, why wasn't Peedy there today?"

"I dunno, maybe he was afraid those two tough guys would show up again."

Fortunately the two tough guys were nowhere to be seen for the rest of the week. Peedy later filled us in as to why. "I found out that those guys only come over to Midland one day a week for shop. The rest of the time, they go to that old school over on Kennedy Road." The mere mention of that school sent a shiver down my spine. Billy had gone there last year when he got kicked out of Midland.

The source of this vital information about the Kennedy Road boys was, as usual, Peedy's mother. "I told her exactly what they looked like, and she said she saw them over there when she was helping the doctor in-tox-i-cate the kids for mumps and measles." That meant that it was only Monday mornings when we had to worry about the 'mince pie bandits,' as Eddie called them. But what if they showed up on the street somewhere? That could be cause for concern.

Because of the huge snowstorm that Thursday, everyone but me got home late. Nan and Liz were on a bus that got stuck in the snow, and John? Well, he was just late, as usual. As for me, since they closed the school at three o'clock, I made it home at around four and hardly noticed that the car was still in the driveway. Stamping the snow from my rubber boots on the newspapers scattered just inside the door, I yelled out, "I'm home, Mom. We got out early."

"Mama's gone out." This unexpected greeting came from my father, who was getting up from the nap he took every day before going to work. He had emerged from the back hallway in a dressing gown and slippers and stood in the kitchen entrance with a freshly lit cigarette in his hand. Surprises like this one rattled me because Dad always seemed to find some reason to get mad at me. "Don' make such a mess," he said sharply as he looked down at the linoleum floor where the melting snow had pooled. At times like this, I would immediately tense up because I was afraid I wouldn't understand what he was saying. Now I just stood there, speechless and frozen on the spot. I watched him walk to the sink for a glass of water. He stared out the window as he let the tap water run over his fingers. Then, in a slightly softer voice, he said, "How come-a you never say nothing to me, uh?" What could I say? Because half the time, I didn't understand what he was saying? Because he frightened me? But saying something like that now might really make him angry. He filled the glass, took a couple of gulps, and then spoke again. "I'm-a you father, no?" He was looking right at me, his voice rising once again. I felt stupid and embarrassed.

"Yes," I managed to mutter. I had yet to take off my coat or step out of my boots. Why didn't I just turn around and walk out the door? That thought crossed my mind, but I just stood there. I was unable to move.

"Hang up-a you coat, an' wipe-a d'floor," he said. Then, using his thumb and forefinger, he squeezed the burning tip of his cigarette into an ashtray and headed off to the bathroom.

In those moments of helpless humiliation, my father's words confused and saddened me. This man was my father. I was supposed to love him, but

Larry Ricciardelli

he refused to let me. Why couldn't he be nice to me anymore? The way he was just a few years ago when he used to call me, 'il mio piccolo Lorenzo'?

For the first five years of my life, I had Dad all to myself. I went everywhere with him during those precious daytime hours when John, Nan, and Liz were at school. Back then, I wasn't afraid of the strange sound of his voice. Or perhaps it simply didn't matter that his English was so very different from Mom's or Uncle George's. Italian accent and all, I felt safe with him holding my hand when we crossed the street, and I loved sitting beside him in the car when we were alone, just the two of us.

By the time I was six or seven, we'd lost each other. Once I started school, we rarely spent any time together. Most of my friends had fathers who were at home almost every night of the week. But my dad was different. He was gone from our house six nights of the week. From late afternoon until one or two o'clock in the morning, he worked as a dining room waiter at the Orchard Park Hotel in Toronto's east end.

While Dad was getting ready for work on that snowy afternoon, I stayed in my bedroom to practise my penmanship using my new ballpoint pen, a Christmas present from Uncle George. I carried it with me all the time. Mrs. Goode thought it a good idea to keep it handy so that I could practice my penmanship wherever I went. After a while I got to reading a war comic book that Tommy had loaned me. I'd have to leave my math homework until Nan was available to help me with mixed fractions and long division.

Mom got home from a downtown shopping trip just as the clock bonged six. She stomped her feet inside the front hall, and brushed the snow from her coat before taking it off. I waited pen in hand to see if she had remembered to pick up a pad of writing paper. But with barely a word to me, she called out, "Nanette, have you got the potatoes on?"

"Oui Mama, elles sont en train de bouillir," Nan called back from the kitchen.

Plunking her Eaton's shopping bag down on a chair with her coat hanging from one arm, Mom patted me on the shoulder and said, "Busy evening, dear. My sewing ladies are coming tonight. We'll have to have supper right away. The ladies should be here by about half-past seven." In the kitchen Nan put away her school books and began setting the table. "Where's Elizabeth?" Mom asked, washing her hands at the kitchen sink.

"She was upset because Patsy said her hair made her look like a stupid little kid or something, so she's gone over to the churchyard pour se coucher sur la neige," replied my eldest sister without having to look up a single word in French.

"Well, there's no time for 'couchering' or anything else right now," said Mom, opening a can of peas. "Laurence, put your coat on and go and find Elizabeth."

"Aw, Mom, I'm a little tired from ploughing home through those gigantic snowdrifts."

"Oh, your poor sweet thing. Now run across to the churchyard and find your sister. There's a good boy."

Duty-bound and devoted to my mother's peace of mind, I knew this was not the time to bother her about the writing paper. Instead, I zipped up my parka and stepped into my boots warmed by the heat from the radiator which was also where I left my gloves. Sitting right on top of it!

I began my mission through la neige, trekking across the front yard and through the gate where I stopped to gaze out at the vast white land on the other side of the street. I thought about going back for my gloves, but decided just to keep my hands in my pockets. And nestled inside my right pocket was my little ball point pen. I clicked it in and out as I waited at the corner for a car to pass. It trundled along McIntosh Street, its chain-bound rear tires clanking heavily over the rutted snow. The heavy snowfall of the late afternoon had dwindled to light flakes, and the wind had died down to almost nothing.

At first, I couldn't spot Liz anywhere in the churchyard. Then I heard her yelling near the church portico, a good fifty or sixty yards away. "Cut it out, you buggers!" The sound of boys laughing like frontier ruffians forced me to throw caution to the gently falling snow, and I took off, a Siberian husky chasing a herd of reindeer.

As I got closer to the portico, I could see two boys. One held Liz's arms behind her back while the other shoved handfuls of snow in her face. "Liz!" I shouted, and unsure of just how to pull off this daring rescue, I ran out into the middle of the road and began waving my arms and bellowing a desperate cry for help. One of the ruffians let go of Liz and came running towards me. Quickly sizing up the opposition—a lot bigger than me, and at least three, maybe four years older—I immediately took the defensive position I'd learned from Tommy's comic book. HIT THE DIRT (or snow) AND COVER-UP! As I landed, I felt something jab me in the gut. It was my pen, still safely tucked away in my pocket. From the portico I heard, "Drag that kid over here, Bernie!"

As ordered, Bernie dragged me off the road, but I kept one hand in my pocket clutching my pen. "You bastards!" shouted Liz, who was now in the clutches of the other ruffian. "You're gonna get it for this!" With that, she yanked her arm free and made a break for the road. Bernie let go of me and tried to grab Liz as she ran by. "Run, Lolly!" she screamed. I tried to get away, but the other boy was after me as soon as I could scramble to my feet. As he reached out to grab me, I pulled out my pen. With one upward thrust across my chest, I rammed that little ball pointed dagger as hard as I could into the ruffian's hand just as he locked onto my shoulder.

"You little shithead!" he screamed, releasing his grip. At this outburst of vulgarity, Liz put on the brakes in the middle of the road. Her screeching halt surprised Bernie, who immediately slipped and fell.

"What did that jerk just call my little brother?"

"A shithead," Bernie laughed, getting to his feet.

"It ain't so goddamn funny!" the other boy shouted, shaking his pen-punctured hand up and down.

Again, Liz surprised the two bullies by taking a step towards them. "Why you two rotten bums," she snarled, "your language is gutter talk. Cursing like that at my little brother really gets my dander up!" The two rotten bums took a step back as Liz took another one forward.

"Whattaya' gonna do about it?" said Bernie, sounding a little less like a foul-mouthed bully.

"Yeah, ya dumb broad," added his buddy.

At this unseemly remark, Liz opened her mouth and let out a long, loud "Aaahh!" It sounded more like a wail of a wounded moose than a high-pitched scream. Porch lights went on up and down the street. Mrs. Plasket opened her front door and peered out. Bernie and his pal stood frozen on the snow-packed road as if they'd been nabbed in Kresge's Five and Dime with their pockets loaded up with firecrackers.

A moment of silence passed while Liz looked back at the church steeple. Then as she turned to the ruffians, her voice became that of a Pentecostal preacher. "You two snivelling devils will know the wrath of the Lord God of Abraham!" she boomed. More lights went on. More neighbours looked out their front doors. Now feeling the weight of their sins, the snivelling devils tried to sneak away. "Wait, wait, you evil Philippians!" Liz thundered, "Mend your ways, or the witness of Jehovah will strike you down!"

A black Studebaker pulled over. "What's all the racket?"

"These unrepentant sinners tried to assail us!" Liz was really Bible-thumping now. She even went so far as to remind Bernie and his accomplice of the fate of Lot's wife as she fled from the 'twin cities' of Sodom and Gomorrah. "A pillar of salt she became, and a pillar of salt she remains!" This terrifying image was enough for the unrepentant assailants, who immediately took off down the street without so much as a backward glance.

"Kids!" said the man at the wheel of the Studebaker as he drove away, shaking his head. Folks went back inside to their supper and the evening news while Liz brushed the snow from our coats with her woollen mittens.

"Your hands must be freezing," she said.

"Not that much," I said, still gripping my trusty ballpoint. "By the way, where did you learn all those other scary Bible verses? Reverend Foster never talks like that. He just makes everyone sleepy."

"Ever hear of *Faith of Fire*? It's a radio show."

"No. What's it about?"

"I've only listened to it a couple of times. At Patsy's house. Somebody named Pastor Robert Orley is always talking about evil sinners, the wrath of God, all that kind of stuff. Patsy's mom and dad never miss it."

"The *what* of God?"

"I'll tell you later. Come on. We need to get home."

"Yeah, I'm getting kinda hungry and sweaty," I said, pushing back the hood of my parka. "By the way, what's a Philippian?"

"Goliath's tribe. Remember the giant that David killed with his slingshot?"

"Oh, yeah."

Minutes later we were bounding up the back stairs and into the house.

Larry Ricciardelli

"Where have you two been?" Mom asked as we stamped our feet on a fresh mat of old newspapers. "And what was all that shouting about?"

"That was Liz," I answered proudly, "she put a curse on two evil Philippians!"

Although Liz had exhibited a laudable use of scripture in gaining her triumph, Mom was not entirely happy about the story we told at the supper table. "You really must stay away from boys like that," she said.

"But I couldn't help it," Liz protested. "They snuck up on me while I was lying in the snow making angel wings.

John looked up at the clock. "Sorry folks, but I gotta run," he said, gobbling a spoonful of mashed potatoes from the pot on the stove. "Meeting Stan at the Allenby in half an hour. The new Dean Martin, Jerry Lewis picture."

"On a night like tonight? Listen to those snowploughs out on the highway. The theatre may not even be open." Mom took her final sip of tea and got up from the table.

"Ah, but the show must go on!" John proclaimed, wiping his mouth on a tea towel. "See you later."

Mom sighed, and then realizing the time, she exclaimed, "Dishes, everyone! Miss Purcey and Miss Whitlock may be here any minute now."

"Do you think they'll even be able to get here? Il neige de nouveau." Nan peered out the kitchen window.

"A snow storm won't keep those young ladies indoors. They're members of the Diocesan Altar Guild!"

CHAPTER 16
HE WHO CASTS THE LAST STONE

By mid-March temperatures had risen into the forties, a sign that spring was on its way. So we hoped. Throwing snowballs would soon give way to throwing baseballs, but in the meantime, since we had to throw *something*, we threw stones. These little gems lay in the slush at roadsides throughout the neighbourhood. Supply was more limited than it would be in late spring and summer, so we couldn't be too choosy about size and shape.

One mild but overcast afternoon a kid named Willie Tikanen, the newest arrival to the neighbourhood, joined me, Eddie, and Tommy on our way back to school after lunch. As we walked up Midland Ave. Eddie announced that he'd heard Billy would be coming home from the hospital. "When?" I asked casually, despite feeling a knot in my stomach at the mere mention of his name.

"Must be soon because nobody's seen him yet," Eddie said in his usual, slightly abnormal way of explaining things.

"Who told y' ?" asked Tommy, pulling a comic book from his coat pocket as we mushed through the slush on the unpaved road.

"Peedy's mom," Eddie said, "she found out from the school nurse." Another knot in my stomach formed, feeling like a wrench this time. I needed further clarification.

"*Might* be coming back? But not for sure?" I asked, gathering up a haphazard handful of roadside rocks.

"Who's Billy?" asked Willie.

"A crazy kid who tried to burn down Lolly's garage." Eddie stopped short of giving our new friend any further details about the story. He took off when he caught sight of George Roamers holding his daily news conference on the other side of the road.

"He might be crazy, but not as crazy as these guys!" Tommy chuckled as he showed Willie and me a page from the latest edition of *War Stories*. "Get a load o' these goofy commies." He pointed to a pack of soldiers dressed in quilted jackets, wearing hats that bore a single red star at the front. In this story, two American soldiers are firing a belted machine gun at the onrushing horde. "Stupid Reds, a whole bunch o' the crazy buggers just run right in front of a machine gun and get mowed down by the good guys."

"How come they're called Reds?" asked Willie.

"They're commies, *red* commies. Come from Russia, China, Korea. Places like that. My dad says they're tryin' to take over the whole world."

"How does he know?" Willie pinged a stone off a garbage can in a nearby driveway.

"Because he was a captain in the Marine Corps. Was your dad in the army?" Tommy asked still keeping his sights on the comic book commies.

"Yeah, he was. The Finnish army." Willie threw another rock at the same garbage can. I turned and looked at the field on the other side of the road. My dad wasn't in *any* army. I hoped Tommy wouldn't ask about him.

"Yeah? So what did the Finnish army do in the war?"

"Fought the Russians."

"No kidding." Tommy was impressed enough to look up from the comic book. "Well, like I said, those Russians are no-good commies."

My brother had told me that Russia was on our side during the war, but I decided not to mention that because it might get Tommy talking about Italy being on Germany's side. It was too complicated, and for me it would be undoubtedly embarrassing.

"Just so you know," Willie put in, "there's a lot of people from Finland in Canada."

"So, you're telling us that you came here from Finland?"

"Yeah, I told you my dad was in the Finnish army!" That was something I really liked about this new kid. He didn't beat around the bush about anything. He asked straight-forward questions and gave straight-forward answers. I also liked that his dad, just like mine, was born in a foreign country, as was his mother.

"Well, okay then." Tommy went back to the comic book. "Look at this!" he grinned. The next panel showed one of the Americans holding up an empty machine gun belt.

"We're outta ammo, Sarge! Whatta we do?"

"Fire rocks at 'em!" yells the sergeant.

The last panel stretched right across the bottom of the page. It showed the two bulletless G.I.'s winding up like baseball pitchers and knocking off the enemy with perfect throws.

"Strike three, yer out!" the sergeant roars as he nails another enemy soldier square in the forehead.

"That's stupid," protested Willie.

"What is?" said Tommy, suddenly more serious.

"Soldiers throwin' rocks at other soldiers."

"Oh, yeah ? See that lamp post down there? I can hit it from here. One shot."

"So what? That doesn't mean *soldiers* throw rocks at other soldiers."

"My dad sure did, and he showed me the right way to throw. Watch this." Tommy stuffed the comic book inside his parka, took a stone from his pocket, and wound up like a big-league pitcher. He let the stone fly with a kind of sidearm motion and cracked the post dead centre from forty feet away.

"Okay, Tik, your turn. Let's see y' do *that*." Willie fired with no arm-swinging windup. His shot had the distance all right but was wide of the post by a good four feet.

"Take a shot, Rich," challenged the kid from Michigan, "Tik shouldn't be tough to beat." Confident that I could outdo the wild throwing Finn, I grabbed a stone from my pocket and set myself for a straight overhand throw. Using a slightly shorter windup than Tommy's, I let go with everything I had. Just as the stone left my hand, a tall boy emerged from behind a high fence bordering the corner lot. My shot was off a bit to the left of the post but right in line with the tall kid's head. I heard a slight thunk as the stone struck him just above the ear. He made no sound as he slumped against the lamp post, holding his hand against the spot where I'd popped him. "Geez, Rich, you

Larry Ricciardelli

really corked that kid," Tommy blurted. "Better go see if he's okay." As my two buddies ran to the corner, I stood in the slush watching as the teacher on yard duty ran across the road from the school.

I knew I was in big trouble. I was so obviously guilty of striking down an innocent person. A helpless feeling engulfed me as I watched Mr. Douglas bend over my victim, who now sat in the melting snow at the base of the lamp post still pressing his hand against his ear. After a couple of minutes of quiet talk from the teacher, the boy slowly got to his feet. Then Tommy and Willie lifted his arms over their shoulders, and like three battle-weary G.I.s, they staggered across the road to the schoolyard.

Mr. Douglas waved at me. "I think you'd better come with me, son." I shuffled to the corner, feeling a squishy dampness on my feet. Maybe my boots had sprung a leak. Then as I felt the stones in my pocket, I thought of Liz's story of David, the shepherd boy of the Bible and the enormous Phillipian, Goliath. (Later corrected to 'Philistine' by my Sunday school teacher). Unlike the boy hero who would one day become king, I had been careless in my selection of ammo, and as a result, I had managed to conk someone considerably smaller than a giant and much less dangerous. As a mere commoner, I was sure I would pay dearly for my crime.

Inside the school, Mr. Douglas directed me down the hallway past the nurse's office, where Tommy and Willie were sitting on a bench outside the door. I looked over at them. "He might have to go to the hospital," said the Marine captain's son, looking and sounding about as serious as I'd ever seen him.

On the slow journey to the pricipal's office, I mulled over the various sad scenarios that might materialize. First, I would be judged and found guilty by Mr. Barford, who was still at the wounded boy's side in the nurse's office. My punishment would certainly be the slugs, even if the boy didn't have to go to the hospital. But there was every likelihood that he would be taken away in an ambulance with its siren wailing. If that happened, I would be expelled from school! No 'ifs ands or buts'.

Then there was Mom and Dad to be considered. They would be more than just a little upset by my getting kicked out of school. Mom would cut off my allowance forcing me to find a job, probably in old man Froder's junk yard or with the township garbage department. And Dad? Well I was afraid to even think about what he might do beyond yelling at me in Italian and sentencing me to ten years hard labour in the basement.

Things looked bleak, to say the least. Both Mr. Barford and Mr. Douglas remained in the nurse's office while I sat alone outside the principal's office on the prisoners' bench. I gave a quick thought to saying a prayer, but what could I say to a God who was certain to look with disfavour on one who had cast a stone at a helpless lamp post, missed, and had ended up hitting a young lad, not just in the head, but very close to the temple! Everyone knew a blow to the temple could kill a person. And disfavour from God was certainly nothing to sneeze at. That was something the white-haired Reverend Foster had tried to make clear from time to time in his own gentle way, accompanied by a little finger-wagging.

    A few weeks earlier shortly after Valentine's Day, our Sunday school teacher had read us a Bible story about a boy who suffers from a strange illness that makes his body go stiff, throws him to the ground where he screams and grinds his teeth. Suddenly Billy flashed before my eyes, uninvited, even though I hadn't seen hide nor hair of him since November. Could it be that Billy had the *same thing* wrong with him? In the Bible story, Jesus comes to the rescue as usual and heals the boy. "Isn't that wonderful!" Miss Northy beamed. She then reminded us of how Jesus had performed the miracle, but only after the boy's father had said that he really *believed* that with God, anything was possible.

  Well, if anything was possible with God, then maybe He *did* give Billy whatever sickness he had. Or maybe He had the devil do it! I simply had to talk to someone about all of this. After all, you never knew when 'the man upstairs' might get angry. He could punish you for just about any mistake, big or small. Look what happened to Adam and Eve, for Heaven's sake—just for eating an apple!

  When Sunday school ended that morning, three other kids went up to talk with Miss Northy, who continued telling them how *wonderful* everything was, and I was definitely not in the mood for that. The only kid in the Sunday school class I knew, was Dwight Dankworth, who was pretty much a bonehead, so I'd get no help there. Still, I needed to know if Billy might be the way he was because God was punishing him. Mom would be the person most likely to be of help, followed closely by my brother who possessed the knowledge of someone who already had three and half years of high school under his belt.

The moment I got home, I went right into our bedroom where I found John stretched out on the bed with a large book lying open on his chest. "Where's Mom? I have to ask her something really important."

"St. Thomas' downtown," he said, staring up at the ceiling.

"Okay. Well then, can I ask you something?"

"Nothing big, not right now."

"How come? What are you doing?"

"Studying for exams."

"Lying on the bed?"

"Yeah. I told you, the brain works better when you're relaxed." He continued to stare at whatever had captured his attention on the ceiling. "But at the moment, I'm just taking a break."

"Where's Nan?"

"At Graddi's, I think." My sister had only a year and a half under her belt, but she would have to do for now.

I sat at the kitchen table for a few minutes, just staring out the window. Was it worth the walk down to Graddi's house, or should I wait until Mom came home? Then I heard Dad's radio from the basement. I wondered why he wasn't cooking. It was almost noon and we always had Sunday dinner at one. He'd have to come upstairs pretty soon, and I didn't want to be around to get roped into sweeping the rec room floor or something. Most of all, I sure wasn't gonna ask *him* a question about God getting angry.

My grandmother welcomed me with open arms. "Hello, dear, what brings you down the road to see me on such a gloomy afternoon? A nice hot cup of tea and some biscuits?" Mom and Graddi were so much alike, filled as they were, with comforting words to make you feel better when things weren't going so well.

"I have to talk to Nan."

"I was just about to put the kettle on," Graddi smiled.

"Thank you, Graddi." It was impossible not to be polite with my grandmother. She had to be one of the kindest people I knew. That must have been because she grew up in England when Victoria was queen, at a time when everyone had good manners.

Here in my grandmother's living room I felt so much better than I had just half an hour ago when I was sitting in our own kitchen and hearing Dad's radio in the background. Now the whole Sunday school thing was starting to lose a lot of its steam. After all it *was* just a Bible story. But on the other hand, with stuff like that you could never be sure. It wouldn't hurt to get a little extra Bible knowledge from someone who had already passed their church confirmation test. I perched on the arm of the chesterfield where Nan was sitting with her school binder open on her lap along with her blue French textbook. "I want to ask you something, Nan," I said.

"You, mon petit frere, can ask me anything you like, but I've got something to show you first. Quelque chose tres interessant." She held up a magazine with a picture of a football player on the cover. In the upper left hand corner in large block letters was the word SPORT.

"Did you buy this?" I slid down the arm onto a cushion.

"No, a very nice boy in my Math class told me I looked like this girl." She pointed to a picture of a very pretty girl in saddle shoes and shorts a few pages inside the cover. The caption read: PERT KATHY CROCKFORD HEADS THE CHEERLEADERS AT MICHIGAN STATE "And then, he just gave me the magazine. Said he'd read it a dozen times already. He had the most gorgeous wavy blonde hair. I couldn't very well say I didn't want it." Nan blushed a bit and then handed me the magazine.

"Gee, thanks, Nan." I started flipping pages. What a magazine! It must have had at least ten full-page colour photos. Halfway in, I stopped to look at a picture of a hockey player putting tape on his stick. 'Wild Bill Ezinicki' it said on the opposite page. I thought back to that hockey game I had listened to after seeing *Frankenstein*. How the excitement in Foster Hewitt's voice (John had told me a few things about hockey broadcasting since then) along with the crowd noise, made all my worries about weirdness just fly out the window. And now I had these colour photos with stories about the players. Right away, I felt better. In fact, the 'wrath of God' got put back in the Bible where it belonged!

"Hey, this is the guy that Mr. Staley likes." I showed Nan the picture of the wavy-haired Boston Bruin.

"He must be a good player to be in the magazine, n'est pas? And he's quite joli as well."

"What's that mean? Happy?"

"No, just really good-looking." Apparently Nan liked wavy-haired guys.

The next colour photo was of a baseball player whose white jersey had New York displayed across the front with black lettering outlined in gold! 'The Amazin' Willie Mays' was the banner for this story.

"Alors, what did you want to ask me?"

" Nothing really important. Just some kids' story from Sunday School."

I flipped back to the hockey picture. I figured it this way: since the "clean and fast" game of hockey was the most Canadian sport there was, none of the players could be 'category two' bad guys. Yeah, Wild Bill (not Billy) did have a few scars and a black eye, so I would put him half way between category one and two. And boy, this was a guy who could take care of himself. From now on I would be just like him!

For those few precious minutes I was waiting outside Mr. Barford's office, I was able to bathe in the memory of my first encounter with the heroes of pro sports, and the way I had skated blissfully through the last weeks of February into the less wintery weather of March. Then suddenly I was awakened from my reverie by the sound of staccato footsteps echoing down the still empty corridor. I looked up and saw Mr. Barford exit the nurse's office and begin marching towards me.

"Boots and coat off out here," said the principal upon his arrival. To add insult to my unhappy situation, the zipper of my parka jammed. Though I struggled mightily to get it unstuck, my sweaty fingers could not unzip the zipper. Finally, I was able to wriggle free of my coat by pulling it off over my head. Further humiliation tracked me as I stepped out of my rubber boots and found soggy pieces of newspaper insoles stuck to my socks. "Inside," said Mr. Barford, evidently heedless of the embarrassment I was feeling. He closed the opaque windowed door and immediately took to his swivel chair. Wheeling it into place behind his heavy oak desk, he pointed to another less comfortable-looking chair in front. "Sit," he said as he opened one of his desk drawers. My heart skipped as I watched him remove a shortened black leather belt from the drawer. He then placed it carefully, almost reverently, on top of his green desk blotter. The only other items on his desktop were a pen and pencil set, a pad of paper, and a large black copy of the Holy Bible. A very neat and serious-looking desk.

This was my first in-person look at the much-talked-about slugs. It looked a bit like the one that hung down the side of Mr. Staley's barber's chair. Slightly narrower and thinner perhaps than the ones used to sharpen razors, this one was obviously designed to inflict swift and biting pain on the hands of reckless and disobedient pupils.

"Well," said Mr. Barford, sounding surprisingly calm, "what do you have to say about this, Laurence?" I kept staring at the black punishment, trying to gauge its sting. "It looks quite useful," I said quietly while rubbing my weather-reddened hands on my knees.

"I don't mean this," he said, tapping the strap with the tip of his fountain pen. I glanced up for a second and caught him grinning slightly. "I mean, what do you have to say about hitting young Derk in the head with a stone?"

Unable to purge my imagination of the punishment I was certain awaited my poor hands, I gathered myself into a spirit of humble but eloquent contrition. The words came out quite effortlessly thanks, in great part, to Billy Northcott and his college-level vocabulary. "I apologize to young Derek, to his mother and father, and to you sir, for the harm that I have caused." A glimmer of hope arose from within as I looked up momentarily and noticed that Mr. Barford's grin had broadened just a little.

"Well, I'm sure his family will accept your apology. Fortunately, *Derk*, not Derek, by the way, is not seriously hurt."

"Thank the powers that be," I said just above a whisper as I lowered my eyes once again.

"But you have broken an important rule," continued Mr. Barford as I resumed rubbing my rubbery knees, "a rule made to protect us from the careless behaviour of others." He tap-tapped the desk blotter with his fountain pen.

"Such as throwing stones?" I offered compliantly.

"Exactly. It's not that you should never throw stones, but there are places where it is simply not allowed, specifically anywhere near the school." Then taking the strap in hand, he leaned back from his desk. "The breaking of an important rule requires an appropriate punishment," he continued as he rocked back and forth. "Do you understand?" He enunciated each word crisply, then leaning forward, he placed the strap squarely in the centre of his desk.

"Yes, I understand, sir. You've explained it quite nicely. But I'll listen quietly if there's more to be said." This brought yet an even broader smile to his face.

"And so to your punishment," he said, clearing his throat and picking up the strap again. "Stones can be extremely dangerous, as I'm sure you now realize. In fact, in biblical times, people were often punished for serious crimes by being stoned to death." He tap-tap-tapped the Bible with the tip of his pen. I was now bent so far forward in the chair that I was practically kneeling on the floor. "You must understand just how dangerous and deadly stones can be."

Raising my folded hands, I said with every ounce of honesty I could muster, "Yes, oh yes, I do see the danger and death in every stone that lies silent on the road."

"Good. You've clearly learned the first part of your lesson, and I must say you have quite a way with words."

Seizing the compliment, I pressed on with honesty and eloquence, drawing on a limited store of occasionally inspiring words from the Reverend Mr. Freeman. "Thank you for your grace and forgiveness, sir. You have lightened the yoke of my burden." This last statement brought to the principal's face the biggest smile yet. "And may I also say that I've learned that a stone must be cast upon the waters far from the lilies of the fields." This little gem sent him rocking back in his chair with a hearty laugh.

"Well, well," he said, pulling his chair up to his desk, "you do seem to have a good grasp of biblical language, in a manner of speaking. So, I think we'll incorporate that into your punishment."

"I'm not going to be stoned, am I?"

"Oh no," he laughed, "but come to think of it, that does seem rather appropriate somehow." He paused for a moment, and then, tapping the Bible twice, he said, "Instead, you will read selected passages from this great book to your two friends every day after school for a week."

"You mean I have to read the Bible out loud? With Tommy and Willie listening?"

"That's the idea," said Mr. Barford, placing his hand firmly on the Bible. "Tommy and Willie also broke the same rule, but it was your stone that struck young Derk."

"I understand, sir. I did indeed cast the last stone."

"That is why you will do most of the reading. But don't worry. I'll be here to help. Yes, indeed, we'll make biblical scholars out of all three of you. Now off you go to your classroom. And remember, 'A stone cast among the lilies of the field is a stone not left unturned.'" Mr. Barford chuckled as he leaned back in his chair. "Oh and, tell the other two boys to come in." Outside the office Tommy and Willie sat on the bench, heads down.

"Okay Guys, your turn," I said quite matter-of-factly.

Upon our release, the three of us slogged through the school yard with snow falling in heavy, wet flakes. "A whole week o' readin' the Bible," Tommy grumbled. "I woulda taken the slugs any day. At least y' get it over with."

"Sorry, I just figured the best thing was to sound really pitiful the way they do in the Bible."

"Well, I'm real sorry you're so pitiful!" the Marine Captain's son growled and stomped off to catch up with big Gordie Cosgrove.

Our tripartite alliance with the Michigan native evidently on shaky ground, Willie and I soldiered on by ourselves. "I hope you're not mad about the Bible reading," I said.

"Nah, they only read the Bible in Finnish at our church, so I guess hearing it in English won't be too bad. And I'm sure glad we didn't get the slugs. Tommy says it makes your hands bleed."

I felt the stones in my pocket. "I coulda killed that Derek kid, y'know, if I'd got him in the temple. See any blood on his head?" "Nah, just a bump behind his ear, and we never heard him yell or anything in the nurse's office."

Larry Ricciardelli

The snow began to fall harder, and the wind picked up as we turned down McIntosh Street.

"Well, I'm still worried. I mean if he never made a sound, maybe I damaged his brain or something."

"Don't worry. My brother Edwin got knocked out cold when he was twelve when a brick fell on his head. But he's in university now studying to be a doctor." Boy, that made me feel better! I mean, knowing that even if a brick falls on your noggin, it doesn't mean you're going to die or get brain damage.

"Wait a minute," I grabbed Willie by the arm. "How come a brick fell on him?"

"Helping my dad build a house. Tell you about it later. Let's go to my place and listen to *Sergeant Preston of the Yukon*."

"Yeah, okay."

Then, "On King! On you huskies!" we cried as we ran across the churchyard.

CHAPTER 17
UNEXPECTED CONSEQUENCES

The next morning, Mom got a call from Mr. Barford, who filled her in on the full story, including the punishment he'd imposed. She was not particularly pleased because all I'd told her was that I'd accidentally hit a boy with a small stone, but he wasn't seriously hurt. I hadn't even mentioned going to the principal's office.

"Well," she said when I got home for lunch, "Mr. Barford tells me you're going to be reading the Bible after school as a way of reminding you and your two friends about the rules of safe behaviour."

"Yeah, I mean yes, Mom. I was going to tell you that part later."

"You should always divulge the entire story, Laurence. Telling only half the truth isn't really telling the truth at all." She poured herself a cup of tea while I tucked into my customary noon hour soup and sandwich.

"I know, but I didn't think it was all that important." I downed a large spoonful of delicious, nutritious tomato soup.

"Do you really think that being sent to the principal's office isn't important?"

"Well, yes... it is, but..." I broke off and went into the coughing, stalling routine.

"All right, you can stop the coughing now and start being serious."

"I am being serious. I think I might be getting a bit of a cold." I sniffed once for good measure.

Mom just looked at me as she blew into her teacup. Then, with a hint of a grin, she said, "Do you think it might be a good idea if I called the doctor?"

"I think I'll be okay." I blew my nose on one of John's handkerchiefs, which Mom insisted I carry with me in the wintertime.

"At any rate," Mom went on, "I think Mr. Barford has the right idea. And since it would seem that you may have a talent for reading the Bible, I think it would be a good thing for you to learn something about church music as well."

Unsure I'd heard my mother correctly, I paused before swallowing a mouthful of peanut butter and banana. "Church music? What's that got to do with reading the Bible?"

"When I was your age, I found that reading the Bible helped me become a better singer in our junior choir."

"Well, I don't think I could be as good a reader as you were, Mom. And besides, I'm not even in the choir. I'm not old enough. Could I have a cup of tea, please?"

"When you've finished your lunch, all of which you are to chew and swallow properly, by the way. As for being too young, Mrs. Broadhurst is starting a summer choir just for children.

"A real choir?" I looked up, trying to gather myself in the face of the catastrophe I could see beginning to unfold. "One that you sing in at church on Sunday mornings?"

"Just for the summer months. We'll see about the regular choir in September." Mom refilled her teacup.

"I just don't know, Mom," I said quite calmly. "I'm not sure choir singing is my... uh, cup of tea."

"Now you know how much Nanette and Elizabeth enjoy the choir at St. Aidan's." Mom finally poured me some tea.

"Then they should join Mrs. Broadhouse's choir too."

"They're too old, I'm afraid. It's just for children under twelve. And the name is Mrs. Broad*hurst*, not *house*." Although I knew it was next to impossible to change my mother's mind when it came to church matters, I still tried on the off chance that a reasoned argument might sway her, if presented properly.

"You know, Mom, we learn a lot in school every day, and at Sunday School as well. And we learn even more from our mothers at home. Isn't there just so much learning a person can take?" I added two heaping spoonfuls of sugar to my tea.

"No amount of learning is too much, dear." She smiled and took a small sip of tea. Small sips usually meant tough arguments.

"As you know, Mother, the good scripture reader depends heavily on his voice, and I'm afraid singing in a choir might strain my vocal cords."

"Choir practices don't start until June, and your Bible reading should be over long before then." Another small sip.

"What about Scouts? I can get on the waiting list now and be ready when they have space. But if I have to go to choir practice, I won't have time for much else." I was well aware that Mom was keen on my joining the Scout troop since John was already a top-level King's Scout.

"Oh, I'm sure you'll find time for both, and besides, your singing will need to improve before you can join the troop." I failed to see the connection between singing and scouting, but when Mom got up from the table to wash the few dishes sitting on the counter, I sensed that it was futile to pursue further logical argument. I would now have to plead for mercy, my one remaining defence.

"Mom," I said with my voice cracking just a bit, "you know those frilly collars that choir boys are forced to wear? Well, somebody told me they're really uncomfortable and might even choke you. They're so tight! And they're also very hard to clean." I took a final gulp of tea and immediately took my cup, soup bowl, and plate to the sink.

"We can all stand a little discomfort now and then," she replied, "and I'm sure your collar will wash up quite nicely in your grandmother's new spin-dry washing machine."

"Where's Dad?" I asked. My father's unpredictable mood made it risky to bring him into any discussion, but in this case, I had to take a chance. As a non-Anglican, and a non-church-goer of any stripe, he just might be willing to go to bat for me in this situation.

"He's still at the lumber yard, I should imagine," Mom said as she wiped the kitchen table. Dad always seemed to be somewhere else, even on the rare occasion when I needed him.

Larry Ricciardelli

"Oh, here comes Willie up the driveway," she added looking out the kitchen window. "Better get your coat on."

"Okay, but now my throat feels a bit sore."

Mom just smiled as she handed me my seldom-worn gloves. I zipped up and walked silently out into the gloomy late winter afternoon.

CHAPTER 18
THE LANE

The Easter holidays, eleven days in total, began on Good Friday, whenever that day appeared on the calendar. In 1951 our springtime holidays came during the last week of March, which meant it was still too cold for baseball, but mild enough to turn the ice on the hockey rink to mush. It was just Eddie, Peedy, and me for the first few days since Willie was up north with his dad looking for a place to build a cottage. I didn't see much of Tommy either. He was still pretty steamed about the Bible reading punishment, which he said was entirely my fault. All in all, it was a fairly uneventful week off school except for Thursday.

"Only four days left," Eddie groaned as we walked down the laneway behind Kingston Road that afternoon. "They should make Easter last longer or have it at a time when it's nicer outside."

"Can't change the time of Easter," Peedy said, looking up at the dismal sky. "It goes by when the moon is farthest away."

"Who told you that, your mother?" I said, peering down into the ditch that separated the lane from the backyards of the houses along McIntosh Street. A stream of brownish water moved in fits and starts through the ditch, which sometimes became an accidental repository of valuable items.

"No, my uncle. He's a weatherman at *The Toronto Daily Star*," Peedy said turning his attention to the ditch.

"That paper?" said Eddie, kicking slush into the stream. "The stinky Star?"

Before Peedy could counter that barb, I cried out, "Hey look, a fifty-cent piece!"

"Grab it quick before it disappears!" Eddie pushed my shoulder. Then, as I bent down to fish the coin from the water, a voice from behind us almost made my heart stop.

"Having fun, boys?" Eddie and Peedy turned around right away, but I remained motionless, staring down at the slow-moving stream. How could Billy be standing there without one of us noticing him?

Eddie spoke first. "Hi, Billy… uh, where y' been?" Peedy took a peek at his Mickey Mouse wristwatch but said nothing.

"Oh, just away for a while." Silence. Then, "What have you three been up to lately?"

Kicking at the bits of debris around the ditch, I let my boots do the talking until I could find words. "Not much." I put the large coin in my pocket and fingered my ballpoint pen. Always there just in case.

"We heard you were in the hospital," Eddie said. "Peedy's mom told us. Right, Peedy?"

"Uh, yeah." Peedy looked at his watch again. "I have to go downtown with my mom. I better get…"

Billy broke in with a laugh. "That's funny, Peedy. I should have known it was Nurse Wilson who spread the news." I brightened a little at hearing him sound more like the Billy I first met way back last summer. "Well, I *was* in the hospital for a few weeks at the beginning," he explained, "but since Christmas, I've been staying at my aunt's house out in the west end."

I finally turned around to see him leaning against a tree trunk just a few yards away on the opposite side of the lane. "Didn't see you come up the lane," said Eddie taking a few steps towards the other side.

"Came down from the highway." Billy pointed to the alley between Willard's grocery store and the hardware.

He smiled at me, and I was drawn to him just as I was before. His blond hair was slick and neatly combed. His bright blue eyes sparkled even under the overcast March sky. I loosened my grip on the pen. What made me feel really good was that he displayed no signs of weirdness. Was he now just a normal kid like us? With God (and doctors, I guess) anything was possible.

"How do you like my new jacket?" he grinned.

"Pretty sharp," said Eddie.

"Nice," I added. Though I still wasn't quite sure what to make of Billy's surprise appearance, I couldn't help but be impressed by the jacket. It was the same kind I'd seen a couple of my brother's friends wearing: cream-coloured leather sleeves with a navy blue zippered front and the collar turned up at the back.

"It's a good day for staying inside," Billy said. Though still shy of his thirteenth birthday, he looked every bit the teenager. In addition to the jacket, he wore a neatly pressed pair of maroon-coloured trousers and oxblood loafers. No rubber boots or galoshes for Billy Northcott! The new jacket didn't surprise me, but why would he be wearing a pair of dress pants on a day like today? "Why not come over to my place and watch TV?" he suggested.

If we all went together, I thought, it might be okay, so I crossed over to the other side and stood beside Eddie while Peedy hung back close to the fence.

"*Howdy Doody's* on in a while."

"Can't right now," Eddie said, "my violin teacher's comin' over at four."

Billy smiled as he looked across the lane at Peedy. "What about you, Mr. Fence-sitter?"

"My mom's probably already at the bus stop waiting for me." Peedy checked his watch one last time, then climbed the fence and was gone.

"Well, you and I can watch TV by ourselves then, Lolly." I flinched remembering Mom's warning from the summertime: *I don't think you should be alone with that boy.*

"Don't know if I can," I said weakly.

Back down the lane, a rough-running truck with a rusted-out muffler turned in off Sandown Avenue. It rumbled and shook as it navigated the slush-filled ruts and rolled ponderously in our direction. "We could look at some really old *Mandrake* comic strips I found in my aunt's basement," Billy suggested, seemingly oblivious to the racket and the smell of thick black smoke pouring from the truck's exhaust pipe. While he maintained his casual pose in front of the tree, Eddie and I kept staring up at the old crate with its open box piled high with rusty scrap metal and old tires. As the truck bumped up and down, a couple of the beat-up tires toppled from the mountain of junk, and one after the other, they splashed down heavily in a large puddle no more than five feet in front of us. Eddie and I jumped back but still got soaked up to our knees. Billy, however, was stuck in front of the tree and couldn't escape the deluge. His new jacket and sharp-looking pants took the brunt of a wave of slush, mud, and cold water.

The truck stopped. A kid about sixteen jumped down from the running board to retrieve the tires. He looked up at Billy. "Holy shit, did you ever get a soaker," he laughed, "yer drippin' all over with mud n' crap." Then with the strength of a lumberjack, he hurled the tires up on top of the junk pile and got back into the cab. "What a fuckin' mess!" He laughed as he rolled up the window, and then with another eruption of black smoke the old crate trundled off to Froder's junkyard.

Billy stood in silence with splotches of brownish wet snow dripping from his cheeks onto the upturned collar of his jacket. He was, in a word, a mess from head to toe. I looked at him but didn't move, as frozen as you can get standing in a puddle of slush. "Geez," said Eddie, taking a tentative step towards him, "are you okay?"

"Do I look okay? You moron!" Billy's pants looked like they were soaked right through.

Head bent down, Billy's words now became a mixture of fear and anger. "My mother's going to kill me. She'll whip me again. I know she will!" I started to get that same sickening feeling I had when Billy told me about blacking out at the restaurant last summer. In a series of short, jerky breaths, he sobbed, "It's a-a-all your fault. I came look-looking for you to tell you that I'm fee-ee-ling better, but-but look at me now." Suddenly his tears turned to rage. "You," he screamed, glaring at me, "you're to blame!"

Eddie took a step back, "C'mon, let's go."

"Go on! Run away like everyone else!" Billy shouted. I just kept staring at him, this sad and angry kid who was at once so compelling and terrifying. How could we leave him there covered in all that crap?

"Billy," I said with surprising calmness, pulling out one of my brother's handkerchiefs, "Here, you can use this to wipe off..."

"I don't want your stupid snot rag! It's too late for that!" He wiped his runny nose on the sleeve of his jacket and looked down at the mud. "Oh, you were my friend all right," he sniffed, "until your mother said 'No'." Then came a couple of quick breaths before he started shouting again. "You lied to the police and told everyone I was crazy. I'll get whipped for sure, but... but *so will you!*"

Eddie dashed to the other side and scrambled over the fence. "C'mon!" he yelled. Billy lunged. I turned, made it to the fence, and was partway up when he grabbed my parka, practically ripping off the right pocket. I pulled free and had one leg over the top. Billy made one more lunge but lost his grip on my left boot.

I left Billy standing in the lane, apparently unable to scale the wire fence in his no-traction loafers, maybe afraid that he might tear his slush-soaked trousers. Now I ran as fast as my squishy boots would carry me through someone's backyard, past an old outhouse, and out onto the street. Eddie and I stood on the sidewalk, breathing hard. "What happened?" Eddie said, pointing to my torn pocket.

"Billy... oh, no! My pen's gone." I stuffed my hand into the left pocket and patted the rest of the parka, hoping I had put my little ballpoint dagger somewhere else.

"What about the fifty-cent piece?"

"It's gone too."

We looked back at the lane. Billy had retreated to the far side and stood once again in front of the lifeless tree. Suddenly he spotted us, and holding my pen in his clenched fist, he shouted, "I've got this, and I'm going to get you too!"

I said nothing at suppertime about what had happened in the lane. When Mom asked me how my parka had gotten torn, I told her it got caught on a wire fence. Not exactly the truth, but at least I'd told her the correct location. "And why aren't you eating your pork chop and mashed potatoes?" she asked.

"Upset stomach," I moaned.

"Quite likely too many sugary Easter eggs this week," she concluded after I turned down a bowl of rice pudding. I quietly disappeared into the bedroom. Thankfully John was out somewhere, so I had the radio all to myself. But sadly, even my favourite radio shows failed to erase the images of Billy in his mud-splattered new jacket, yelling across the lane, "I've got this, and I'm going to get you too!" My pen, I suppose, was the least of my worries. At least I knew where it was. However, as frightened as I was by Billy's threat, I couldn't tell Mom or anyone else about how crazy he'd acted. If she or my

Larry Ricciardelli

brother went to speak to Mrs. Northcott, it would only make Billy madder, maybe crazier, and I'd be on the run every day.

The only thing that saved me from a near sleepless night was a book. It was one that Nan had borrowed from the library the day before. "I brought you this book, mon petit. Nancy Foster read it when she was your age and absolutely loved it."

"What kinda book?" I asked, not particularly thrilled at the thought of reading a whole book with thousands of words and probably no pictures at all.

"C'est un roman incroyable! An adventure story about four kids and a magic ship."

That sounded pretty good as actual books go, but as a kid whose twelfth birthday was still a couple of weeks away, I was still more interested in comic books and sports magazines. And although I'd pretty much given up on *Mandrake the Magician*, I continued to read everything else from *Combat Casey* (one of Tommy's Korean War heroes) to *Donald Duck*. So I said "Merci beaucoup" to my sister and left the book on my bedside table.

I lay there for a while, trying my hardest to listen to *Rescue Squad,* but I couldn't shake the terrible thought of running into Billy tomorrow or the next day. Finally, with my interest in that night's adventure of Hal and Sal waning, I clicked off the radio and picked up the book. I spent the next few minutes examining the book itself. It didn't feel too heavy, had a lovely blue cover, and its pages were still tightly bound. Inside there were pen and ink drawings on several pages. Better than I'd thought. But it was the smell that really hooked me. It was like a mixture of library paste and vanilla pudding, almost good enough to eat.

I began to read. *The Ship That Flew* was not at all like the fairy tales that my grandmother used to read to me. For one thing, the story took place in modern times and centred around the adventures of a boy about my age named Peter. Peter lives outside an English seaside town with his younger brother and two sisters. One day, while in town for a dentist appointment, he discovers an old store he's never seen before. The store owner, a kindly old man with a patch over one eye, sells Peter a toy sailing ship that has magical powers. It can grow large enough for Peter to ride in, and even more amazing—the ship could fly!

As I read about Peter's journey home in his wonderful ship, I put all thoughts of Billy to rest. By the time I'd reached the fourth chapter, I felt I had found a new and trustworthy friend. I slept soundly that night after all.

CHAPTER 19
A FRIEND, INDEED

Friday, the last of our days off of school, turned out to be a gorgeous early spring day. A sky full of bright sunshine chased away the grey clouds that had hung around for most of the week. It was a good day to get my bicycle out of the garage, where it had been hibernating since late November.

"Goin' over to Willie's, Mom," I said, pushing aside a ton of winter coats in the hall closet to pull out my slightly squashed spring jacket.

"I thought he was up north," Mom said as I headed into the kitchen.

"Came back last night." I pulled out a couple of crumbled cookies that had spent the winter in my jacket pocket.

"Well, don't forget to tidy your room sometime today. You know how Dad feels about your leaving things in a mess. And speaking of mess, you might as well deposit those moldy old cookies right in here." She popped the lid of the kitchen garbage can.

"Okay. Where is Dad anyway? Outside?" I hesitated before turning the doorknob.

"He's at the hardware getting the saws sharpened." The coast was clear. Out the back door and into the sunshine, I whipped into the garage and grabbed my bike, which was leaning against the back wall. The tires looked okay, and though I didn't want to hang around dusting off the seat and the handlebars in case Dad came back, I still paused for a second to glance at the burn marks on the wall just inside the garage door. It was funny how Dad never said anything else about that incident after the police left to pick up Billy. Yeah, well with both Dad and Billy, you could never be sure what they'd do. And if Billy was still anywhere around, I didn't want to get caught flat-footed, so I took a running start down the driveway, jumped aboard, and pedalled my old fender-less CCM as fast as I could up Sandown.

Just outside the church, I spotted Ronnie Northcott, Billy's half-brother, who played in the floor-hockey league in the church basement every Friday. "Hey, Lolly," he called out as I came roaring up the sidewalk that was now cleared of snow and mostly dry. I screeched to a stop in front of Ronnie, who stood with his hockey stick over his shoulder. "I hear my brother went a little crazy on you and Morrow yesterday," he remarked in a fairly matter-of-fact way.

"Yeah, he did, sort of," I said cautiously. "Is he okay?"

"Yeah, for now anyway," he said with a slight grin. "But who knows what he'll be like next week?" He thunked his hockey stick into a mound of melting snow at the edge of the road. "Anyhow, he's gone back to Mimico. This time for good."

"For good?" I watched Ronnie break off a chunk of crusted snow with his stick.

"Yeah, pretty sure." That was good enough for me.

"Did your mom get mad at him for getting his jacket all crapped up with mud n' stuff?"

"She sure did! Got an earful from my dad too." He stickhandled the snow chunk on the sidewalk, then fired it at the church door. "Wish they'd buy me stuff like that. That jacket musta cost at least fifteen bucks."

"Do you think Billy's really crazy? I mean, like an insane person in a mental hospital?"

"I dunno for sure, but like they say, 'He's goin', goin' and maybe even gone!' Who knows?" Ronnie walked away laughing, but I didn't crack a smile. It just didn't seem right that his own brother (even half-brother) thought it was funny. Somehow, I felt sorry for Billy even though he scared the heck out of me. After all, he was still just a twelve, going on thirteen-year-old kid.

I saddled up and pedalled into the driveway of the first house past the church. Willie was sitting out on the back steps whittling a stick. "Whatcha doin'?" I asked, dropping my bike in the middle of the unpaved driveway.

"Makin' a spear," he said, working away with his tongue stuck firmly to his upper lip. "Good for huntin' groundhogs at the cottage."

"Geez, I could have used a spear like that yesterday."

"Yeah, why?" Willie looked up and flicked his penknife closed.

"I was hangin' around with Eddie and Peedy, and we ran into Billy Northcott in the lane."

"Who?"

"You know, that crazy kid I told you about."

"The one who tried to burn down your garage?"

"Yeah, that's the guy." I sat down beside my friend as he examined his handiwork, looking down the shaft of the spear with one eye closed. I filled Willie in on the details of our laneway encounter and told him what Ronnie had said just a few minutes earlier. "So anyway, Billy's gone back to the hospital. This time for good." I leaned down to grab a few stones from the driveway.

"I guess you're happy about that, huh?" Willie got up and stepped out into the driveway.

"Yeah, I sure am, but I still feel sorry for him… kinda."

"Why? I woulda punched him in the face if he tried to grab me."

"Yeah, but you never know what a crazy person will do if you try to fight back."

"Don't worry about him so much," laughed the Finnish boy. "I'll scare him off with my spear if he ever comes after you." With that, he hurled his newly-carved weapon half the length of the driveway where it neatly pierced a small pile of snow beside the garage door. "How big was the truck in the lane? As big as ours?" Willie pointed to a red, half-ton Chevy pickup parked just to the left of where the spear had landed.

"A lot bigger! Old man Froder musta had five tons of junk piled up in it."

At that moment, a large, white-haired man wearing a red, flannel hunting shirt opened the door. "Viljo," he said in a loud voice followed by a stream of words I did not understand.

Willie turned and looked up at his father. "Okay, Esau." He then ran down the driveway to retrieve his new hunting weapon. "Gotta go help my dad," he called back.

"Doin' what?"

"Cleaning up a coupla lots over near Kennedy Road."

"Is he gonna build houses over there?" I was hoping Willie would ask if I could go along to help.

"Yeah. They'll probably start diggin' in a week or two." Willie carefully placed his spear under the stairs.

"Gonna be home in time for *Sergeant Preston*?"

"Think so. See y' later."

I picked up my bike and walked slowly back out to the sidewalk. New houses. Yeah, I could still remember Dad taking me over to watch the builders in our old neighbourhood when I was about four. But now, he seemed too busy working on the rec room or the garage to take me anywhere. Maybe it was because we didn't know what to say to each other. Willie was so lucky he could speak Finnish. What if I could speak Italian like Dad? Nah, he'd probably still get mad at me for no reason at all.

I headed back down towards Kingston Road. At the corner, I heard, "Hey, Lolly!" It was Willie leaning out the window of his dad's truck. They turned right and drove off along McIntosh Street. I stood for a moment with one foot on my start-up pedal, looking down the street towards Billy's place near the end of the block. Funny that I'd never even been inside his house and never got to see his big television. Probably never would, not after what happened yesterday.

Then I spotted Dad in our driveway carrying lumber out of the garage and piling it up alongside the fence. Figuring he'd see me for sure if I went past the house, I waited until he'd disappeared into the garage, then I made a run for it. My tires zip-zipped through the rivulets of melting snow along the side of the road as I whizzed past our place and down to Tommy's house on Kingston Road. I figured he must have gotten over the Bible reading by now, and I knew for sure he'd be as happy as a pig in a poke about Detroit finishing the hockey season in first place.

CHAPTER 20
A GREAT SUMMER ON THE HORIZON

April 16, 1951, was a Monday. That day marked the completion of the first dozen years of my life. A mere five days after I'd blown out the candles on my birthday cake, I was proud to say that the Toronto Maple Leafs had won their fourth Stanley Cup in the last five seasons! But Tommy's power-packed Red Wings, the defending champs, didn't even get past the semi-finals. And to make things even better (at least for me) Billy had not been spotted anywhere in the neighbourhood for over three weeks.

Now that it was ninety-nine percent certain that Billy would be gone for a good, long time, I was able to concentrate on my school work. I was at the peak of my game in Arithmetic and Penmanship, and received an A+ in both subjects on my final report card. To top that off, I'd placed second in the township junior handwriting contest. Mrs. Goode had been so pleased with my performance that on School Awards Day, she pinned my work on the main bulletin board just below the King's picture and right beside Mr. Hudson's, chairman of the Scarborough Board of Education. My teacher had inscribed my work using red ink: *Neatness in penmanship is next to sporting excellence on the playing field.* "If you ever become an Olympic athlete, Laurence," she said to me that day, "remember that the strong hand which grips the javelin is the foundation for the same nimble fingers that guide the pen." On the way home Eddie said he had no idea that handwriting was an Olympic sport. Peedy and Willie got a big laugh out of that.

Larry Ricciardelli

The fact that Billy was still in possession of my little ballpoint pen made no difference to my penmanship performance since the rules of the contest at the junior level, allowed the use of "pencils only." I still had not told Uncle George that I'd lost the Christmas present he'd given me.

The only black mark on my record was the stone-throwing incident back in March, but Mr. Barford had assured me that that in itself would not prevent me from passing into Grade Seven. "Just keep up with your regular Bible readings and count your blessings," he told me.

Count my blessings I did. Number one: Billy's absence from the neighbourhood for the foreseeable future. Number two: the raise in my allowance. And number three: a very pretty girl named Sally who joined our Sunday School class on the first Sunday after Pentecost. I was one lucky twelve-year-old, but I was also a near teenager with a couple of added responsibilities. Since my weekly stipend had shot up from fifteen to twenty-five cents, more horticultural chores were added my schedule. I was tasked not only with caring for Graddi's garden, but also with digging up dandelions and such from our own vast front lawn. Along with these labour intensive, boring jobs, came a less-than-thrilling summer activity forced upon me by my mother—singing in the junior church choir!

CHAPTER 21
YOU HAVE GOT TO BE KIDDING!

It was at Uncle George's outdoor birthday party on an otherwise glorious Saturday afternoon in late June when Mom went public with the announcement. I was caught completely off guard because Mom hadn't mentioned the choir at all since that dismal day back in March when she first brought it up. Uncle George, himself a member of the adult choir, was tickled pink that his youngest nephew was about to join the ranks of Anglican choristers, albeit for a limited period of time. With a smear of whipped cream clinging to his ample moustache, he announced, "We'll have you singing Gregorian chant in no time at all. Have another piece of strawberry shortcake!"

"One step at a time, George," Mom interjected. "Learning the hymns will be plenty to start with."

Learning hymns in the summertime? Good God!

When we got home that afternoon, Mom decided I needed to know what was expected of me starting the very next week. She read out my marching orders from last Sunday's church leaflet.

"Registration for the Summer Children's Choir will take place on Monday, June 25th at four p.m."

"Can't you tell me this tomorrow?" I moaned, flopping down on a kitchen chair. "I have to meet Tommy and Willie up at the park."

"Your father and I will be spending most of tomorrow at Mrs. Bonner's farm out in Clarkson, and I may not have time to explain everything. So

Larry Ricciardelli

Tommy and Willie will just have to wait. I want you to be absolutely sure about where and when to register." But it was the last part of the announcement that was the real killer. "Practices will be held every Friday evening from six forty-five to seven forty-five." A whole hour of practice right when *Tom Corbett, Space Cadet* was on the radio!

My poor head clunked down on the table. "All choir members are expected to sing at Sunday morning services during July and August."

"Every Sunday?" I slid off the chair and collapsed in a helpless heap on the floor. "Oh, really, Laurence, your histrionics are going a little too far. Now please, up off the floor and try to look at this reasonably. Just think of how choir practice will improve the quality of your voice." Dutifully dragging myself back up into my chair, I sat silently, trying my hardest to imagine gaining any benefit at all from choir practice. I mean why did my voice need improving, anyway? I was only twelve, for crying out loud, and I had no desire to become an opera singer or something just to make Dad happy!

Though nearly worn into submission, I had to make one last plea. "Mom, I promise on my honour, I'll practise singing at home. I'll even sing in the bathtub. You can coach me."

"Now you're being ridiculous, Laurence. Your singing practice will be done at the church on Friday evening." Case closed!

The only thing I could do now was confine myself to solitary until I could figure out what to do. On that day, solitary meant the second branch of the climbing tree on our front lawn, a spot that had given birth to some of my brighter ideas, like goalie pads made out of potato sacks stuffed with rags and old newspapers. Though ideas came sparingly that afternoon, the perspiration flowed freely when I thought about how hot it would be in a long black choir gown with one of those awful, frilly collars around my neck. In desperation, I briefly considered falling out of the tree and enduring the agony of a broken arm. But then I figured even that wouldn't do any good. They'd just tell me to hold the hymnbook in my other hand. A broken leg? Uh-uh. Too drastic even for this dilemma.

Aside from some sort of serious injury, I could come up with no other solution. I would simply have to surrender to a summer of unspeakable drudgery. But wait! Out on the street, I spotted John walking down from Kingston Road. If anyone could help me find a way out of my dilemma, it would be my big brother. Composer of songs, creator of comedy routines, and most recently a jet aircraft designer. Well, at least he did have some kind of summer job at A. V. Roe, the airplane factory where Uncle Dick had a job in upper management.

I dropped to the ground. "Hey, John," I called out as he came up the driveway. "Got something I have to ask you."

"Okay, but it'll cost you."

"What?"

"Just kidding. But I have to sit down . . . hiked all the way from Birchmount."

"How come?"

"Lost my streetcar transfer. Bus driver said I had to pay the regular fare."

"That's life," I quipped.

"Yeah, but I'm tired." That meant that now was *not* the time for a comedy routine.

We sat down on the front steps with the late afternoon sun shining through the trees that bordered the lawn. "You know what? Mom says I have to be in some stupid kids' choir. For the whole summer!" At first, my brother said nothing. Instead, he took a Nielson's Burnt Almond chocolate bar out of his shirt pocket and leaned back. He smiled as he peeled back the silver paper. Maybe he didn't understand my problem. "I can't go in the choir, John. I just can't! What am I gonna do?" John took a generous bite of the softening dark chocolate and handed me the rest of the bar. Finally, he spoke.

"I saw the most gorgeous girl on the streetcar," he sighed, "she must be a cheerleader." I was obviously not getting through to him. We both knew there were no cheerleaders in a kids' church choir.

"Okay, but I have to go to choir practice every Friday night and sing in church every single Sunday!"

Unmoved, my brother took back the chocolate bar, bit off another chunk and, gazing skyward, he said, "Think positively."

"Huh? I *have* been thinking. For the last two hours!" 'Think positively' was not the wishy-washy kind of advice I normally expected from my brother. Right now, I needed the guy who said I could count on him like an adding machine.

He paused his chewing of the chocolate bar to offer what I hoped would be a kernel of wisdom. "But have you thought about what good might come from your stint in the choir?"

"No." I leaned forward, frowning with my hands cupped around my chin.

"They might give out free chocolate bars or... Hey! You might meet a pretty girl."

"A pretty girl? I don't think so . . . No, wait! Maybe, just maybe you might be right." I looked at my brother, who was now chewing chocolate, eyes closed and smiling into the sun. "Sally!" I shouted, "maybe Sally will be in the choir. Oh boy! She's already in Sunday School, and there's no classes in the summer, so maybe..."

"No maybe about it. She *will* be in the choir. You can count on that!" John opened his eyes as he licked the remains of the Burnt Almond from the wrapper. "Oh, by the way, it's well known that most girls love chocolate. Now let's go see what's for supper."

CHAPTER 22
AND THE ANGEL SANG

The following Monday, I joined a group of two boys and five girls in the largest of the three basement Sunday school rooms. A teenager named Tim Bothwell, Mrs. Broadhurst's assistant, was in charge of our little choir of eight. I knew the two boys from Sunday school, Dwight Dankworth and Ellery Mason. The group of girls, however, contained nary a familiar face; there was no Sally or anyone even remotely resembling her. After about ten minutes I began to give up hope and considered telling Tim Bothwell that I was going home because I felt sick and didn't want to spread whatever I had to the others. Who knows? I might have polio. I mean, I couldn't just say I was sick at heart. As I was about to go up to the older boy to tell him I was packing it in, I remembered my brother's bold statement: "She *will* be in the choir. You can count on that!" She was probably just late getting here. I would wait for half an hour and then plead sick if Sally didn't show up.

Our first task was to print our name, address, and other important stuff on a small card using equally small pencils. Dwight and I had to share one of these little stubbies, which Tim Bothwell assured us would be replaced later in the month by brand new full-length 'writers,' as he called them. "Boy, am I glad!" Ellery said through gritted teeth. "These things make your fingers go numb."

"The church provides what it can, when it can," Bothwell proclaimed. "Be thankful for small mercies and tiny tools."

"He sounds like my grandmother," Ellery smirked as the older boy went to answer a knock at the door. I held my breath as the door swung open.

"You didn't have to knock," Tim said cheerily as a girl with dark pigtailed hair entered the room. This was definitely not the fair-haired Sally I was hoping for.

"I'm sorry, sir, but I wasn't quite sure where I ought to go. Is this where I'm to join the choir?"

"Yes, come in. You can sit right over here." Bothwell escorted her to a chair opposite to where Ellery, Dwight, and I were stationed. "Oh sorry, what's your name?"

"Mary Thorne."

"Nice to meet you, Mary. We're all filling out our registration forms. Name, address, and telephone number, if you have one."

"Now he sounds like our principal," Ellery murmured.

"Yeah," I said absently. "And *she* sounds like Princess Elizabeth." I gazed dreamily at the new girl who was dressed in a dark blue tunic, like the one's Nan and Liz wore in gym class, only a bit longer.

Mary completed her form and handed it to Tim in exchange for a little blue hymnbook. She sat quietly humming while the other girls whispered among themselves. I was sure I could hear the sounds of *All Things Bright and Beautiful* coming from across the room, and then she looked up and smiled at me. At that moment, all thoughts of Sally vanished. When she looked my way again, her eyes shone, and in the dank air of the basement room I was left savouring the sweet smell of lilacs and roses. Suddenly, this marvellous moment was blown away by Bothwell's booming voice. "Finish up quickly now." He looked over at Dwight, Ellery, and me. "Mrs. Broadhurst wants all of us upstairs in five minutes. It's showtime!"

Dwight was still scribbling away with our shared stubby. Together we had managed to flatten its lead point into a wooden scratch. My focus though, was elsewhere, cloaked as I was in some sort of velvet fog.

"Jesus loves me," I whispered quite involuntarily.

"What?" said Dwight, leaning sideways.

"I know why I'm here," I sighed.

"So do I," Dwight snapped. "We're supposed to be signing up for choir, and this stupid pencil won't write anymore!"

"You're an angel," I murmured, staring across the room.

"You're nuts!" barked Dwight. Giggles erupted from the girls, and more fragrance drifted towards me from Mary's smile.

Neither of us spoke to each other that first day. In fact not a word passed between us for an entire month! What could I say to a princess? To a girl who had come from another world? And yet her bright eyes and sweet smile continued to send silent messages to me, keeping me on cloud nine all through the first weeks of summer.

One afternoon, Willie and I were tossing a ball around at the park, waiting for Tommy to get there with his hardball bat. "Wanna go fishing with me and my brother on Sunday?" Willie asked.

"Yeah... uh no, maybe not. I have to be in church."

"Too bad. I won't be goin' to church this summer at all once my dad finishes the cottage." Willie threw me a palm sizzling fast ball.

"Oww! Take it easy, will y'? This stupid glove doesn't have any padding!"

Willie grinned, "Come on up to the cottage and chop some wood. Make your hands tougher."

Well, there would be no trips to Willie's or any other cottage for me that summer. My hard-throwing pal, on the other hand, would head up to Lake Harrington in a few days and stay there for the last six weeks of summer. As much as I envied Willie for his summer at the cottage, I took a smidgen of solace in doing my duty to Mom and Mrs. Broadhurst. But it was Mary, a singing angel, who made me count the days to the next Friday night practice.

One rainy August evening, just before practice, I was granted a small glimpse of heaven when Mary uttered her first words to me. "Can you tell me what this means?" she asked in a voice that seemed to come from somewhere over the rainbow. Her delicate hand held up her hymnbook, and with a gentle finger, she pointed to the word, 'spheres.'

Totally unprepared for a question of this complexity, I responded thick-headedly, "What?"

"This word," she repeated, tapping the page lightly. "What's its meaning?"

Again, the only word I could muster was another sluggish sounding, "What?" The princess was about to turn away, no doubt thinking me some kind of moron with a vocabulary of a single word, when, thank the Lord, a peel of thunder cracked open my foggy but fertile little mind. "That word," I blurted, "means spear, like the thing you throw at somebody."

"But it's not spelled that way," she pointed out with majestic clarity. This called for a quick but reasonable explanation.

"That's the way they spelled it in the days of the ancient Philippians, who were sometimes called Philistines," I declared with scholarly confidence. "And the music of the spears is the whistling sound they make when you throw them."

"That's quite a lovely explanation. Yes, I understand now." Then she softly sang, "All nature sings and round me rings the music of the spheres… Your name is Lolly, isn't it?"

"Yes, but my real name is…" I answered a little awkwardly, but she smoothly filled in the gap.

"Lolly sounds such a happy name. It rhymes with jolly." Suddenly it was Christmas, 'time for mistletoe and holly.' Mary smiled at me once more before turning back to her hymnbook. The sound of my name on her lips made me weak. I had become like the cradled child of Bethlehem. I remember nothing more about that stormy Friday night.

Sunday turned out to be the hottest day of the entire summer. A day when the junior choir would be seated at close quarters with senior choir members in the little chancel of St. George the Guardian, Anglican Church. Along with the ninety-degree temperature, came Bishop Small on his summertime visit to one of the smallest church buildings in the diocese. For this reason, Mrs. Broadhurst would not yield on the issue of the wretchedly uncomfortable frilly collars. "Have to wear them, ladies," announced Tim Bothwell, who called everyone 'ladies' or 'people.' "The 'bish' is big clergy. We pull out all the stops this morning."

"If he's big clergy, how come his name is Bishop Small?" Ellery Mason made one of his usual disrespectful, wise guy comments.

"You, mister," Tim barked, "just button your collar up straight and button your lip, too!"

"You tryin' to get booted out?" said Dwight Dankworth, who had his surplice on backwards.

"Yeah, I am. The only reason I'm here is because my grandma says I have to be."

I, on the other hand, was now quite happy I'd joined the choir and so, I would be pulling out every stop I could, not just for the "bish" but for the girl who would be sitting directly in front of me in a few minutes. I'd been so excited that morning that I could barely choke down a single spoonful of cornflakes. As we lined up at the back, along with half a dozen or so members of the adult choir, including Uncle George, I began to feel a little queasy. Then Mary turned and smiled at me. An instant Pepto-Bismol!

We processed up the aisle, flanked on either side by a larger than usual summertime congregation. I sang out my praise lustily. But by the time we'd filed into our places, the queasiness had come back, and I could hear my stomach rumbling while we listened to the collect for the day. "Please, Lord," I prayed silently. "Don't let her hear the gurgling in my loins or whatever the Bible word is for stomach." With each canticle and scripture reading, the temperature seemed to go up a degree or two, and by the time everyone stood up for the Gospel, I was sweating like a Gadarene swineherd. The queasiness in my loins had risen to the level of pukiness. Now the temperature inside the packed church felt like a hundred degrees. And to make matters worse, the Gospel passage was that same familiar story about the demon-possessed boy that had frightened the heck out of me when Miss Northy read it to us back in the wintertime. As Reverend Freeman read the description of the poor boy in the grips of a mouth-frothing seizure, I could feel my thumping heart speed up. Little dots suddenly jumped up in front of my eyes. "I feel dizzy, like I'm gonna faint," I whispered to Dwight.

"Well, sit down," he whispered back, tugging at his tight frilly collar. Instead, I gripped the back of the bench in front of me, determined to stay upright at all costs. The reading mercifully came to an end, but almost immediately, Mrs. Broadhurst launched into the next hymn, *Stand Up, Stand Up For Jesus*. I was still standing but for how long?

About halfway through, I could feel an on-rush of saliva pouring into my mouth, and the dizziness got worse. At the same time, a picture of the raging gospel boy materialized in my head. What if I became just like him—shrieking wildly and throwing myself on the ground? The words in my hymnbook began to bounce all over the page. The sweat on my forehead was icy cold, but the rest of me was on fire. I fully expected to hear a voice like the one Billy heard that night in the restaurant. All I could do now was to offer up a silent prayer for the hymn to be over. But Mrs. Broadhurst's rotund figure kept pounding away at the organ. The up and down motion of her arms and white surplice sent waves of nausea across the chancel, crashing into my churning stomach. And then came a voice, the sound of someone whispering in my ear: "Alone, alone, lost and alone!" Spoken in a rhythmical pattern those few fearful words so overwhelmed me that my own voice completely disappeared. Helpless to utter a sound and nearly paralyzed with panic, I was certain that I'd been stricken with lockjaw. My knees turned to jelly. I reached over and grabbed Dwight's arm, but he shook me off, leaving me once again clinging to the back of the bench. Barely moving my lips, I managed to whisper one last prayer. "Please, oh please Lord, don't let me pass out and end up puking all over the angel princess!"

Then a sliver of hope appeared as Bishop Small began his slow approach to the pulpit. At the same time there arrived a miracle for the ages! Weak and on the verge of collapse, I heard a second voice: "Don't worry, Lolly. You're not going to faint. Everything's going to be all right." It was the voice of an angel, Mary's voice! At that very moment, the organ and the singing stopped. The panic, the awful dizziness, and the cold sweat all seemed to evaporate at the same time.

In the pulpit, the bishop bowed his head. "May the words of my mouth," he solemnly said as I relaxed my grip on the back of the bench. Off-balance now, I grabbed the sleeve of Dwight's oversized surplice. "And the meditations of all our hearts," continued the bishop. Thud! I sat down hard, dragging Dwight down on top of me. "Be always acceptable in thy sight, O Lord." The bishop paused for a moment, an apparent acknowledgement of the slight ruckus in the second row of the choir. As he began his sermon, which was about the power of prayer in times of need, I sat there like a weary Bedouin at a desert oasis. I was now being bathed by a cool breeze that the Lord had miraculously funnelled through the open window directly behind me. Yes, my little prayer had not gone unanswered.

It was the words of an angel that had saved me. She had saved me from sickness and unspeakable embarrassment, plus the possibility of conking my head on the back of the pew if I'd passed out. So welcome was the relief I now felt that I could have easily dozed off listening to the words from the pulpit, which seemed directed right at me. "Ask, and ye shall receive," said Bishop Small. "The Lord God Almighty has always been a source of strength to those who are sick or grievously troubled in any way." You can say that again!

After the service, I stood outside mulling over what had happened a little less than an hour before, eternally grateful that I had survived the ordeal. When Mary came out the front door, she looked a little worried as she walked towards me. "Are you all right?"

"Sure I am. Why?"

"I heard you thump down just as the bishop was starting his sermon. What happened? Did you feel faint?"

"No, no. I was just kinda tired. And hot. I didn't get to sleep until late." A good, nothing-out-of-the-ordinary explanation and partly true.

"Oh," she said, bending down to tie the laces on one of her highly polished brown shoes.

"Do you know anyone who has television?" I asked, changing the subject to something more interesting.

"No, we've only just arrived here from England. And oh, I see my father waiting for me over there." She pointed to a tall man on the other side of the street, smoking a pipe.

"Okay. See you next Friday?"

"Hope so." She smiled again and ran across to her father.

CHAPTER 23
DON'T CRY JOE

Friday arrived with rain again, late in the afternoon. Could this be a sign? I thought back to our last practice, the night she asked me about 'spheres,' the only time we really ever had what might pass for a conversation. What was it about rainy evenings in the church that made talking with a pretty girl so exciting? The shadowy chancel? The pitter-patter of the raindrops? Would this be another magical Friday? If Mary got there a little early before most of the other kids, what would we talk about? The king? English cars and Dinky toys? Or what it's like having bombs dropped on your house? Mulling over these topics, I shovelled in as much creamed salmon and canned peas as I could manage before jumping up from the table. "Well," said Mom, "look who's eager to get to choir practice. No time for dessert?"

"Lots to practice. Gotta pick up some stuff on the way over." I was out the door in a flash and with a running start I hopped on my bike.

First, a stop at Mr. O'Brien's because, "It's well known that most girls love chocolate." I grabbed a Nielson's Burnt Almond and two Crispy Crunch bars, put them up on the counter and waited for Mr. O'Brien, who was on the phone as usual. Why is he on the phone so much? I wondered, fishing a couple of dimes out of my pocket.

"Three tonight? Would y' be sharin' the sweets with a young lady?" I blushed a bit as the friendly Irishman picked up the money from the counter. He stretched the phone cord to its limit, keeping the receiver pressed to his chest.

Larry Ricciardelli

"Do y' want something else?" he said, about to drop my twenty cents into his cash drawer.

"Not sure."

"How about some baseball cards? Since you're a good, God-fearin' lad, I'll give y' two packs for the nickel. Your friend Tommy buys them six at a time."

"No hockey cards?'

"Not for another two months or so. What'll it be, lad? Cards or your five cents change?"

"Okay. I'll take 'em."

My knowledge of pro baseball was still limited. I'd read about Willie Mays in the magazine I got from Nan, and I'd heard of Babe Ruth, of course. Tommy had told me that he played a long time ago and was the greatest home run hitter of all time. Oh, I knew the rules all right since we played softball at school. So I was on solid ground for handling any questions Mary might ask about baseball. After all, everyone knew that cricket was the only game with a bat and ball they played in England.

As it turned out, neither baseball nor cricket would matter much that night because Mary Thorne was nowhere to be seen. What's more, I found it near impossible to hide my disappointment, suffering as I did even through a mercifully shortened practice of forty minutes. In between hymns, I sat hunched over on the bench, chewing my fingernails. Standing up, I kept looking over at the door and hoping. Halfway through practice, I surrendered to a series of sad probabilities: She probably doesn't really like me. She was probably being kind, like most English people. If she thought I was a nice kid, she would be here tonight. Somehow, she must have found out that Dad's Italian, and everyone knew that Italy and Germany were allies for most of the war. To make things worse, Dwight kept grinning and whispering stuff to Ellery. I was sure they could tell I was 'down in the dumps,' as Graddi would say. Talk about feeling alone! Finally, after what seemed like half an hour of overtime practice, Mrs. Broadhurst glanced at her watch and said, "Oops, we're a bit later than I'd planned, but before you leave, a word from Tim about this coming Sunday."

"All right people, Mrs. Broadhurst has already told you how marvellous you were last Sunday for the bishop, so we're going to let you dress down a bit for this week's service. Girls, leave your beanies at home, and boys, you get a break from the frilly collars. Questions?"

"So we don't have to wear the stupid... I mean, nice little collars?" Ellery was still trying to get himself kicked out and, at that moment, I wished that I'd had the nerve to say something like that too.

Before Tim could retaliate, Mrs. Broadhurst said, "Good night, everyone. See you bright and early Sunday. And don't forget, all things *are* bright and beautiful."

Thanks to Mrs. Broadhurst's reminder, I couldn't get that hymn out of my mind. I kept picturing Mary humming the tune the first night I saw her. As I pedalled up the lane behind Graddi's house with still a good hour of daylight left, I thought about stopping in to see her when I heard the crack of a bat. Kids in the vacant lot had resumed play after a two hour rain delay.

It was not quite a year ago when Billy and I ended our friendship there. I remembered the baseball game that day. How I'd picked up the ball and thrown it back to one of the kids. Then I thought about Mary again. Cricket and baseball. Maybe I'd see Mary again, maybe I wouldn't. But baseball was a definite thing. You could count on it being played somewhere by somebody every day in the summertime.

And in my pocket were the two packs of cards which, in my rush to get to choir practice, I had all but forgotten. Now seemed like the right time to see what I had. Powdery pink bubble gum to start with, and then my first ever pro baseball card! I stood for a moment, staring at the picture. A ball came bounding over the weeds and rocks, out of the lot and into the lane. I picked it up as it rolled towards a mud puddle. Holding my cards in one hand, the ball in the other, I looked up. Someone shouted, "C'mon, throw it!" The ball was a little wet but I fired it back anyway, over the head of the kid in right field. Then taking a second look at the card, I yelled, "Hey! You guys know who Mickey Mantle is?"

CHAPTER 24
HOPE SPRINGS IN AUGUST

When Mary came back to church unexpectedly for the very last summer service, a bubble of hope rose from the bottom of my floor-length cassock. She walked gracefully into the choir room, attended by the aroma of Rose of Sharon. Feeling a blush coming on, I quickly looked down to avoid being ribbed by Dwight, who delighted in making a mockery of the slightest thing you did. As we waited for Tim Bothwell's command to march forth from the choir room, she tapped my arm with her little hymnbook. "I have something to tell afterwards," she said.

"And I've got something to show you!" How could anyone not be impressed by the lineup of baseball players I carried in my shirt pocket?

"Shush! Every one ready?" Tim walked reverently to the front of our little group with the cross held firmly at eye level.

"Ready for what?" Ellery never gave up. Even with only two weeks left, he still wanted his dishonourable discharge.

"That's enough, mister." Substitute crucifer, Bothwell turned and scowled at the unrepentant choir boy. I on the other hand, was now quite happy in the service of Mrs. B. and her assistant. With five of my best cards tucked safely away in my shirt pocket, I was already planning my after-service chat with the girl who was walking up the aisle directly in front of me.

Happily deep in thought for the entire service including the recessional hymn, I tripped coming down the chancel steps and partially lost my right shoe in a humiliating fall from grace. Nevertheless, I managed to shuffle down the aisle as Mrs. Broadhurst hammered out her version of: *Christian, March Boldly Into The Fray.*

I was so excited to get out of my choir uniform that Sunday that I barely heard Tim Bothwell as he boomed out, "Don't forget the soiree, people. Mrs. Broadhurst's back garden at four this afternoon." I would try to remember for later, but right now, I was headed for sunshine and lollipops.

I waited under the big maple in the churchyard, trying to appear relaxed, maybe even "cool" as my brother and his friends would say. I would start with Mickey Mantle. He was still young but from everything I'd found out about him, he was destined to become a great player. Plus, he had the looks of a movie star!

Mary appeared a few minutes later, looking a tad more serious than she'd been when she came into the choir room. Maybe something bad had happened. I tried to smile, but something was wrong. I could tell.

"There's something I really should tell you. Can we talk for a short while?"

"Okay. Uh... let's go up to the park."

We sat on the grass in the middle of Sandown Park, an area one block wide and half as long. At the north end stood the boards of the natural ice hockey rink, which served as a make shift hardball diamond for eight months of the year. You got credited with a homer by 'hitting one out' over the end boards. Softball was played on a regular sized diamond backed by a chain link screen at the south end. There was already a game in progress there.

Not sure exactly what to do or say, I gazed silently at Mary for a bit and imagined us sharing a Sweet Marie chocolate bar. Then glancing down towards a group of guys at the softball diamond I thought, those guys don't know what they're missing.

"Do you like toffee?" she asked.

"Yeah, I mean, yes. Sure!" She traded me candy for Mickey and a player to be named later.

"Who is he?"

"A baseball player. Keep him if you like. This is great toffee!"

"Oh, he looks so young. And a little bit like you." She shielded her eyes as the sun emerged from behind a passing cloud. I stopped chewing.

"You... you look like, uh... Judy Garland." She blushed and suddenly leaned forward and kissed me on the cheek. I was gone! Off down the yellow brick road.

She took my hand and brought me back. "Would you like to kiss me?" she said ever so softly. Speechless, I nearly choked on the toffee. "Well, silly Billy?" She closed her eyes. The moment our lips touched, I found myself in a bright new world where everything was possible, and I was afraid of nothing, not even silly Billy Northcott.

"I can taste your toffee," she said.

"So can I," I murmured. I felt her squeeze my hand, and then she let go. Suddenly she toppled sideways, sprawling onto the grass, staring up into the sun. She had scrunched my Mickey Mantle card, although she didn't seem to have hurt herself in any way. Geez! Did one little kiss do that to her?

"Mary?" She blinked but said nothing. I gotta get some help! "Hey! Come 'ere, will y'?" I yelled at the softball player in centrefield, but he trotted towards the infield to catch a lazy fly ball. I waved frantically, but didn't even get a look in my direction! I turned back to Mary. She was moving a bit and seemed to be coming around.

"Oh, dear," she said in a slightly groggy voice as she propped herself up on one elbow.

"Are you okay?"

"I think so. How long was I...?"

"Maybe a minute." We sat for a bit without saying anything. Then she looked at me.

"I'm sorry, I wanted to tell you about this before."

"Oh, don't worry. I'm not upset or anything. I'm just glad you're okay." I glanced at the crumpled Yankee right fielder lying on the grass beside her, but Mickey would have to wait.

She explained that her three-week absence from the choir was due to her "condition." In other words, it had nothing to do with me. She told me that the doctor had given her some pills to take when she felt faint or really anxious in a place like church or school or anywhere at all for that matter.

"Anxious? I thought that meant being excited. Like, you can't wait for the Saturday matinee or Christmas holidays."

"It also means nervous, even frightened for no reason."

"Really?"

"Yes," she nodded, "but the sun *is* a little too much for me right now. I think I should be going."

"Can I walk you home?"

"That would be awfully nice." She managed one more sweet smile as she took my hand.

By the time I had walked Mary to her aunt's house over on Kennedy Road, she had told me a lot about her condition.

"They don't know what causes it. Perhaps too much sunshine or any very bright light can set it off. But the worst that can happen is that you might have a fainting spell, which can be a little embarrassing. But your truly good friends will still be your friends."

I thought I might tell her about Billy. Were his spells the same thing? No, I decided. I'd talk to her about that some other time.

Mary kissed me on the cheek a second time while we were standing behind a tree across from her aunt's house. "I hope we'll be good friends, Lolly. And oh, I *am* sorry about your baseball card."

"Oh, that's okay. I can get another one. That toffee was the sweetest ever!"

She walked across the street and from the front door she blew me a kiss. I was so happy, I could have fainted on the spot!

CHAPTER 25
THE RED LIQUORICE SCARE

Monday, with only a week of summer holidays left, I was feeling crappy, but in a sick kind of way. And the heat! It just would not let up. I mean staying in bed or just *on* the bed when you've got a headache and when the thought of food makes the blue sky turn green, well that could very well turn into a hideous day for any twelve-year old. And this, the day after Mary's kisses had sent me on a rocket ship to the moon! Everything had worked out so well on Sunday afternoon, even after her fainting spell.

But that was yesterday. Today was quite another kettle of pickles, as they say in England. Not only was I home sick on a no-school day, but I would also have to spend most of that day alone. Mom was getting ready to go downtown, and Dad had taken a lunch hour shift down at the White Castle. (But then I probably wouldn't have been any happier having him at home.) Meanwhile, Nan and Liz were spending the last week before school on a farm up in Haliburton. And with John still toiling at Uncle Dick's airplane factory, I would be flying solo until suppertime. But if I had to go through this on my lonesome, then so be it. After all, I would be only two years away from high school starting next week!

I tried going outside, figuring the good ol' climbing tree on the front lawn would offer some shade and maybe a cool breeze. I'd just got nicely settled on the grass with the August issue of *Blackhawk* when old Mrs. Naylor from next door spotted me. "You look like you might have polio," she remarked, setting her watering can down. "I think you should go back inside. It could be serious, you know." She wiped her hands on her apron and added one final less than optimistic comment. "You're just the right age to get it, sonny." She delivered that line like the Wicked Witch of the West: 'How 'bout a little fire, scarecrow!' That was enough for me. I mean, you never know, the well-meaning but nosey Mrs. Naylor might just go and call an ambulance or something. I headed back inside.

No sooner had I gotten in the door, than I went from headache and sick stomach to feelings of I-think-I'm-going-die! Maybe. Despite my troubled state of body and mind, I approached my mother with as much calmness as I could muster.

"Mom," I croaked, walking slowly into the kitchen, "I feel really pukey. I'm a little dizzy, and my throat hurts too." Then deciding that 'polio' might be too terrifying a word, I suggested a more mundane diagnosis. "Do you think I might have the mumps?" A common illness that would not frighten the daylights out of my mother.

"You may have a bit of a temperature," Mom said, placing the back of her hand on my forehead. "But it's not the mumps," she concluded as she gently kneaded the flesh underneath my jaw. "Well, back to bed for a while. We'll see how you feel when I get home." So, it wasn't the mumps, but still a 'bit of a temperature,' could very well mean that I was coming down with scarlet fever or typhoid or maybe even the dreaded disease that Mrs. Naylor had warned me about. Add to that, something was definitely wrong with my eyes, which seemed to be growing weaker by the minute.

I shuffled back to the bedroom, trying to imagine what it would feel like to be encased in an iron lung. Short of breath and wheezing, it was all I could do to climb back onto my bed. Mom poked her head in the doorway, "Lie still, dear, and for heaven's sake, don't worry. I should be back from Harcourts by about four."

So Mom's leaving me sick and feeling worse by the second! Doesn't she care about me? Didn't she read in the newspaper about the boy who went to bed with a stiff neck and woke up dead? Could that happen to me?

After half an hour or so of lying motionless on the bed, my feverish brain got me to thinking about the times I'd fainted. That time down at the Bluffs and then just a couple of weeks ago when I nearly passed out in church. And now, as a shadowy haze was beginning to descend all around me, I wondered if I really *was* somehow afflicted with the same strange sickness that had sent Billy to the hospital. Why did this have to happen now, when I was all alone?

Just as my eyes were about to surrender to the darkness, I noticed the picture of Jesus which hung on the wall beside my bed. Maybe I could make one last effort to say a word to the Lord before something terrible happened. With what little strength I had remaining, I rose and grasped the picture, then immediately fell back on the bed. In the fading light, I looked at the white-robed figure standing in front of a cottage door, one hand poised to knock, the other one holding a lantern. But the more I gazed at Jesus, the farther away he seemed to get. In fact, he was all but disappearing from the picture! Why now, in my hour of need? Is this really how it happens when the end is near?

No, wait! He was still there, sort of. But he appeared to have walked right out of the picture frame! My weakened eyes regained a little sharpness as they followed Jesus from the picture frame towards my little dresser. And then hallelujah! My arms began to recover an ounce or two of strength! I slowly sat up. Jesus was now standing in mid–air, like a 3D picture in a View Master. Then a booming voice filled the entire room: "Go to the mirror. Now!"

I leaped up like I was jumping out of a box of Cracker Jacks, as Jesus muttered, "Does He *always* have to be so loud?" I scrambled to the mirror atop the dresser. There, in the mirror, something else began to take shape. It was like some unseen hand was drawing from the other side of the mirror. First, a metal combat helmet appeared, just like the ones I'd seen in comic books and movies. Definitely U. S. Infantry issue. Then the lines of a face began to emerge, a face that became more familiar with each stroke of the invisible artist's pencil. A beard surrounded a grinning mouth with a half-smoked cigar clenched between a set of gleaming white teeth. Holy N.C.O. ! I was looking at a life-sized drawing of U.S. Army Sergeant, Combat Casey!

"Don't bother turning around, partner. Nobody behind y'. It's just me from the other side o' the mirror. Kinda like you're watchin' me on a TV screen." Speechless, I continued staring into the mirror. What the heck was happening? First, Jesus walks right out of the picture, and then the loudest voice I've ever heard, orders me off my sick bed. Now I'm looking at a comic book character in the mirror! And not just *any* character, but one who placed high in my pantheon of heroes, both real and fictional. In fact *Combat*

Casey was outranked only by *Mandrake the Magician*, Max Bentley, and the Reverend Howard Stuart, curate of St. Swithin's Anglican Church.

I held up the now picture-less picture frame. "What happened to Jesus?"

"Could be almost anywhere. Busy fella these days."

"What about that voice?"

Sergeant Casey nodded upward.

"Really?" I squeaked.

"Now y' didn't really expect a burning bush, did y' ?" He grinned as he puffed twice on his cigar. "But gettin' down to serious business son, listen up real good."

"Yes, sir!" This was the best way to speak to any hero, even though I knew this one was a non-commissioned officer.

"Well, there's a war goin' on over here. Maybe you heard about it on the radio?"

"The Korean War?"

"That's right, partner. We're tryin' to keep the commies from takin' over this whole country. Know who the commies are?"

"Yes, sir. I do, sir. Tommy's dad says they're trying to take over the whole world! And... and they don't believe in God and church n' stuff. Right?"

"You bet. That's why they're called 'godless Communists'. And Tommy's dad is right. Y' see, there's a whole lot of us fightin' the commies over here. But y' gotta understand that they're *everywhere*, son, not just in Korea."

I looked around and gave a quick glance under the bed.

"That's right. They could be anywhere. And believe you me, there's nobody sneakier than a commie! They try to pretend they're just like regular folks, working at jobs just like your dad and Tommy's dad. They're probably right there in your own neighbourhood, lookin' just like ordinary everyday folks."

"But they're really spies?"

"You can say that again, partner. Real dangerous spies!" I was now beginning to think all of this meant something really important. But was it just my imagination? Or the 'bit of a temperature' I had? That thought was quickly dispelled when Sergeant Casey spoke again. "So, here's the deal. Patriotic kids like you have gotta step up to the plate on the home front and start trackin' down commie spies. The bad guys won't suspect kids of goin' after them. So it's your duty son, to start searchin' your neighbourhood right now for suspicious lookin' characters."

"But where?"

"Remember what I told y' ? They're everywhere. Maybe even pretending to be church goers. Now I gotta go, partner. My platoon's gettin' ready for combat. Good luck!" With that, Combat Casey's image began to fade.

"Wait! How do I know for sure who's a suspicious looking character?"

"Commies all love the colour red. So target anyone who wears a lot o' red or stares at a red traffic light for a long time. Oh, and one more very important thing. Keep your sidearm well outta sight."

"My *what*?" But too late. His face had already disappeared from the mirror. 'Sidearm' I would figure out later, but everything else made perfect sense. That's why the North Korean soldiers wore a red star on their hats. Even the Chinese communists who were fighting against us were known as "the Reds." But more importantly, I was chosen to help fight the war right here at home. And I was the perfect undercover agent, an ordinary kid turned commie hunter. And sidearm? Well, sure, that must be my old cap gun. Every kid had one. Polio or no polio, I had job to do.

But hold on! What about the fever, the fading eyesight, the weakness that I'd felt just a few minutes ago? All the signs of sickness were gone. I took one last look at the picture. Jesus had returned to his place, standing in front of the cottage door. "Thank you. Thank you, Jesus," I murmured in a subdued Anglican manner. The white-robed figure turned just slightly, looked up at me, and winked. Any doubts I may have had about miracle healings vanished in that moment. The Junior Christian Soldiers' army needed me, and for that reason, I had been made whole again!

Picking up my sidearm from on top of my dresser and loading it up with a fresh roll of caps, I began to formulate a plan. First, I'd keep in mind Sergeant Casey's advice to his own men. "Use your head, fellas," he'd always say. So start thinking, I said to myself as I squinted through the sights of my six-shooter.

Now let's see… Who are the suspicious people in our neighbourhood? Well, for starters, there's Billy. Funny how just a few minutes ago, I was afraid I was going mental, like him. But now, all that stuff seems so far away, like some kind of bad dream… Who else makes you wonder about what they might be up to? What about Mr. Staley, the barber? He drinks about twenty bottles of coke a day and

Larry Ricciardelli

lines the empties up along that big window ledge. Strange maybe, but no reason to suspect him of being a spy.

Then, as I left the bedroom, I remembered something I'd heard on the radio. It was just a couple of days ago on, *I Was a Communist for the FBI*. "Remember, Philbrick," the FBI boss had said, "their most dangerous ones are the ones you least expect." *Yeah, that's right! It's always the people you trust the most who turn out to be the bad guys... Uncle George, maybe? No, that's impossible. He goes to two church services every Sunday... But what about Mom? The most trusted person in the world! Uh-uh, Sergeant Casey said bad guys, and Mom is definitely not a guy. So, who could be a sneaky Communist posing as a trustworthy neighbour?*

Outside, I made my first crucial observation. It hit me like a commie grenade exploding in your face. Parked across the road was a *red* post office truck. Of course! Who's in a better position to be a spy than someone working for the post office, a person everyone trusts with their mail? In our neighbourhood, that person was the friendly Irishman, Mr. O'Brien, owner of the smoke shop. But he didn't just sell cigarettes and candy. He also sold stamps, took in letters to be mailed, and handled stuff that came in for special delivery.

But hold it a second! I can't just walk in there with a gun stickin' outta my pocket. Another one of Sergeant Casey's rules: never let the enemy know how much firepower you've got. I'd have to make a few sacrifices, like wearing my jacket on a blistering hot day. It was the only way to conceal my trusty sidearm. And so as not to arouse suspicion, I strolled up the street whistling, *The Maple Leaf Forever*. Then I sauntered around the corner past Mr. Staley's barbershop and the alleyway next to the smoke shop / postoffice run by Mr. . . . or was it, *Comrade* O'Brien!?

Inside, I casually walked over to the magazine shelves opposite the candy counter and started leafing through the current edition of *Looney Tunes*. Meanwhile, our trustworthy postmaster stood behind the counter chatting with a customer. It was someone I'd never seen before. Just who was this stranger? And why was he wearing a hat and a heavy overcoat in the middle of summer? And Holy Snot Rag! That's a *red* handkerchief he's wiping his forehead with! I'd have to listen closely to pick up the odd piece of their conversation.

Radio Kid

"So, you have something for me?" asked the customer in a slightly muffled tone. But the accent. It was unmistakable. The man in the long winter coat sounded just like the spies and assorted other bad guys in the movies and on radio.

"Just give me a minute, Mr. Drazen. I'll check in the back room." Mr. O'Brien sounded his usual friendly self, but of course, I knew that all clever spies had to act normally. More importantly, I was aware that I had to do the same. I carefully placed Bugs Bunny and Porky Pig back on the shelf and unbuttoned my jacket. Slight, momentary relief from the steam bath I was soaking in. Even the handle of my pistol was wet with perspiration. The big fan above me provided barely enough breeze to flutter the strips of flypaper hanging down from the ceiling.

I glanced at the cover of the latest edition of *War Stories*. In huge letters, it read: RED MENACE ACROSS THE YALU RIVER! On the shelf below the comic books, a news magazine headline asked: Will the Russians Use the Hydrogen Bomb? More evidence of the Communist plot to take over the world! It all added up: Drazen, a stranger whose voice was a mix of Count Dracula and Joseph Stalin, walks into our neighbourhood post office and speaks out of the side of his mouth. "You have something for me?" This was undoubtedly code for, "Has the package arrived yet from Comrade Malenkov?"

The only other piece of evidence I needed to nail Drazen fell into place just moments later. Maintaining my cover as just another kid at the comic book rack, I picked up the September edition of *Photo Play* magazine. Glancing up, I noticed Comrade Drazen, still alone at the counter, put down a coin and pick up three sticks of red liquorice from a box on the candy shelf. "You're right, Sergeant Casey," I muttered. "The guy chooses *red* liquorice instead of *green* Wrigley's Spearmint gum or even *black* balls. Commies always choose red!"

Now that I had all the hard facts: the foreign accent, the use of the code word "something", plus the red handkerchief, and the red candy, I had to prevent Drazen from getting his hands on that package. I took one last look at gorgeous Ava Gardner and feisty Frank Sinatra in a Hollywood nightclub and placed the *Photo Play* carefully back on the shelf.

Larry Ricciardelli

Okay, here's what we'll do. Fire three shots in the air. Scare Drazen into making a run for it before O' Brien hands him the package. But what do I do then? I dunno, but I have to act fast because Sgt. Casey and Jesus, and maybe even 'the man upstairs' with the crazy-loud voice are all counting on me!

With sweaty fingers, I gripped my slippery pistol as tightly as I could and turned to face the commie. Gun pointing to the ceiling, I squeezed the trigger just as O'Brien emerged from the back room. CLICK! CLICK! A misfire! Ammo must be soaked. Think fast, partner. With my sights locked on a small brown paper parcel in the postmaster's hand, I hardly noticed a third figure enter the store.

Tossing aside my useless .45, I leaped across the floor and was about to jump over the pop cooler when I slammed into what felt like the butt end of a hockey stick. Knocked flat on my keister, I sat there on the floor, shaking my head and staring up at three very surprised-looking men: Drazen, O'Brien, and Mr. Staley, whose right elbow had caught me square in the face. "Hey kid, what's the rush?" said Mr. Staley. "I come into the store for a coupla cokes, and you practically run me into the cooler!"

Struggling to my feet and rubbing the bridge of my nose, I pointed to the parcel. "What's that?"

"This?" said the postmaster. "Well, if you must know, it's a book Mr. Drazen's been expecting for quite some time now."

"That's right, my boy," said Mr. Drazen. "Look, I will show you." He undid the wrapping and held out a book with gold lettering on the cover. "It is a Bible written in the Czech language. Such books are very hard to come by these days." He smiled gently and offered me a stick of red liquorice. I shook my head and looked apologetically at Mr. O'Brien.

Mr. Staley then broke the slightly awkward silence. "You okay, kid? You sure hit me with a wallop, like you were Bill Ezinicki or somebody." With that, he slapped a dime on the counter and then pulled two six-ounce Cokes out of the big red pop cooler. "Gotta run, fellas. There's a kid in the chair waitin' for a brush cut."

"Well, no one's badly hurt," said Mr. O'Brien examining the bump on my nose. "But what were y' thinkin' about Mr. Drazen's package, lad? And boundin' across the floor like a kangaroo!"

"Perhaps the boy thought I was an enemy agent or something silly like that," chuckled the man from Czechoslovakia.

Feeling more foolish by the moment, I muttered, "It was just a silly game. I'm sorry, Mr. O'Brien."

"Is that your pistol lyin' on the floor over there?" asked the Irishman.

"Yes, sir." I walked back to the magazine shelf and picked up my not-so-trusty sidearm.

"And take off your jacket, lad. It must be near ninety-five degrees in here."

With my sweaty jacket slung over my shoulder, I walked sheepishly out the door. From the sidewalk, I glanced back into the store. Through the large display window, I saw Mr. O'Brien pick up the phone while Mr. Drazen opened his new Bible and appeared to read something to the postmaster. So maybe I wasn't wrong after all. Could Drazen's Bible be some kind of codebook? Maybe, just maybe. That possibility made me feel a little better even though I'd bungled my mission. At least I'd found a suspicious person in Mr. Drazen, and there would be others, I was sure. After all, according to Sergeant Casey and the FBI, commies were everywhere!

When I got home, I found the house still empty. Back in my bedroom, I tossed my cap gun into the top drawer of my dresser to rest among my socks and underwear. Then picking up the picture of Jesus I flopped on the bed.

I wonder whether Jesus really healed me? There was no question that I felt better than I did this morning. I kept on looking at the white-robed figure but saw no change. Did he really wink at me just before I went off on my mission? And what about Combat Casey? Was he actually here too? Maybe, but how will I ever really know?

What I now saw in the picture was the Jesus who didn't move from his place outside the little cottage door. I liked that. Someone you could count on to be there all the time. And how about Jesus' mother? Her name was Mary. I liked that too. I drifted off to sleep thinking about yesterday in the park. Ohh, that sweet, toffee kiss!

CHAPTER 26
FATHER, SON, AND?

Dad always took his two weeks of holidays in August. A couple of years ago, he and Mom took the train to New York to visit his brother, Uncle Lorenz. But most often, Dad spent his free time at home, working down in the basement or out in the garage, and visiting friends in the evening. The summer of 1951 was no different. The rec room was still unfinished, but plywood was in short supply, so Dad took time out from carpentry and shifted to plumbing. He was constructing a small washroom down in the basement.

It was the last Friday of the summer holidays. By eleven o'clock, it had gotten way too hot to stay outside, so I retreated to my bedroom to sort out the pile of baseball cards I'd accumulated over the past few weeks. Mom was at Graddi's, using her sewing machine, and Dad was sweating it out down in the basement installing a toilet and sink, apparently with some difficulty. The clanking sound of a wrench on metal pipes made its way upstairs, followed by a booming, "Son-a ma bitch!" I tip-toed through the kitchen and into my bedroom undetected and immediately switched on the bedside Crosley, but not too loud because Dad could hear everything no matter where he was in the house.

The usual few seconds of humming from the radio speaker gave way to the sound of a familiar male voice. It was Johnnie Ray, the singer who made a habit of crying on stage. Right in front of hundreds of people! All the teenagers were nuts about him. But why? As I gazed at Yankee outfielder Hank Bauer, who used to be in the Marine Corps just like Tommy's dad, I just couldn't imagine a grown man crying. Not in public anyway. But I'd seen magazine photos of the 'cry guy' bawlin' his eyes out after singing one of his big hits at The Casino downtown. But this was no time to be thinkin' about guys cryin'!

Let's take all the Yankees we've got so far, and set 'em up in playing positions. Mickey would normally be in right field, but since he's temporarily in the care of Mary Thorne, we'll use Gene Woodling in right… Bauer goes over to left, and the great Joe DiMaggio is in centre… Yogi Berra goes into the catcher's spot, and Allie Reynolds is on the mound… Okay, the guy I just got this morning, Phil Rizzuto, is at shortstop… Name sounds kind of Italian.

"Hey, Lorenz!" It was Dad! What did I do now? "Lorenz, com-a down. I need-a you help."

Did I just hear Dad say he wanted my help? Am I ready for this? Do I have much choice? "Yes" to question one, but "no" to numbers two and three. I mean, I couldn't just take off or pretend I didn't hear him. So I put my six Yankee starters in my pocket and wished myself good luck. Dad called again. "Coming," I yelled back. Alone with Dad for the first time since the winter, I had to act as though I wasn't nervous.

Despite the fact that Dad was whistling while he worked, having apparently overcome any earlier 'son-a-ma-bitch' type problems, I entered the work area with some slight trepidation. It looked like he'd just gotten the toilet bowl bolted into position and was now in the process of hooking up the tank.

"Hold on-a d' nut," he said, handing me a small wrench and pointing to the underside of the tank. As I lay on my back looking up at the toilet tank, I assured myself that it wouldn't be too hard. Right away I spotted a nut partially threaded onto a large bolt coming down from inside the tank. "Looks easy enough," I muttered. "A piece o' cake. Like tightening your bicycle seat." Standing above me, Dad inserted a long-handled screwdriver down into the tank and began to twist the screw while I applied a surprisingly steady hand to the wrench. Done! Dad moved to the other side without a word, still whistling softly. A minute or so later, the tank was securely in place.

"Now open-a tap," he said, looking down into the open tank. 'Open' meant 'turn on' in Dad's way of talking. The little tap was attached to a pipe going into the underside of the tank. I could relax now, so I lay on my back, listening to the hiss of water streaming into the tank above my head. Dad leaned back against one of the cement block pillars and lit up a cigarette. "Good-a work, Lorenz." Those simple words of praise I'd waited so long to hear were like getting Willie Mays, Duke Snider and Sal Maglie in the same pack!

I got up off the floor, eager to be even more helpful. Over by the laundry tubs, on a part of the untiled concrete floor, I noticed the lid for the toilet tank. It looked exactly like the one in the upstairs bathroom. "You want that, Dad?"

"Sure, bring 'im here."

I carefully picked up the oblong piece of white ceramic, handling it as though it were a large serving plate made of expensive china, a little heavier perhaps, but manageable. Dad was peering into the open tank, watching the level of water rise as I crossed the floor clutching my precious cargo. Upstairs the phone jangled. I looked up for a split second and kicked into Dad's toolbox. Off-balance, I teetered to one side and felt myself going down. My grip on the ceramic slab tightened. I managed to hang on, but as I hit the floor, the tank top landed squarely on the nozzle of a blowtorch that was just sitting on the floor minding its own business. A loud crack, like the sound of DiMaggio's bat making contact with a Bob Feller fastball, bounced sharply off the basement walls. The top I'd carried with such care snapped neatly in half, and I was left down on my knees, holding two broken tablets, one in each incompetent hand. I was the accidental Moses.

The phone jangled once more and then stopped. Now there was just silence. Not even a single, 'son-a ma bitch!' The only sound I heard was the soft plunk of something hitting the concrete floor. Out of the corner of one eye, I saw a small shower of sparks and the smouldering butt of a half-smoked Sweet Caporal. I tensed up for what I was sure would be a blast of incomprehensible rage, but I heard only the hissing sound from the topless toilet tank come to an abrupt stop.

I wanted to say I'll try to fix this. But all I could do was to blubber, "I'm sorry. Please don't be mad." If my father was upset as a result of my clumsiness, for some unknown reason, he kept that feeling to himself. Or perhaps he'd unleashed his anger when he threw his cigarette on the floor.

He bent down and took the disappointment from my hands. He placed the broken ceramic pieces gently on the floor. Still kneeling, I continued to sob. Then he took me in his arms. "Don' cry figlio." He held me close, as close as Mom had ever held me. But this closeness was so very different, so rare. I wondered for a moment whether Billy's dad ever held him so close that he could feel the strength and security in his father's forgiving arms and hands or the roughness of an unshaven cheek against his forehead. It was my father's touch that I needed more than anything at that moment.

As I walked away to go back upstairs, I stopped to look back, just to be sure I wasn't dreaming. I turned around at the doorway. He was still kneeling on the floor, rummaging through his toolbox, intent upon repairing the broken tablets that lay beside him. I wanted to watch him do what he did best—work with his hands. But I also wanted to say something to him to let him know how proud I was to be his son. From my pocket, I pulled out the Phil Rizzuto card. "Ever hear of Phil Rizzuto, Dad?"

He looked up at me and wiped the sweat from his dark eyes. "Yeah, he's a good singer, no?"

I smiled as I looked at the action shot of Phil "the scooter" Rizzuto. "You bet, Dad. He's a really good singer."

CHAPTER 27
FRIENDSHIP

"A new year on the horizon," said the Reverend Freeman, "just three months away."

"But that's November," I whispered to Mom.

"He's talking about Advent," Mom whispered back.

Oh yeah, that's about a month before Christmas, I remembered. I always thought September would be a better time to start a new year, what with going back to school, enrolling in Scouts or Cubs, and next year's new cars coming out. That's what Willie liked most of all. He knew more about cars than any of my friends.

So things looked fine and dandy by the time we started school. For one thing Dad was a lot different. He had become so much friendlier towards everyone. Had he softened because I had cried on his shoulder when I dropped the toilet tank lid? Maybe he was just happy to be off work for two weeks. At any rate, on the Sunday of Labour Day weekend, he took the whole family downtown to the ferry docks and then out to Centre Island for a picnic.

What's more, there had been no reported recent sightings of Billy Northcott either on the street or in the school yard. That kind of 'no news' was 'peachy keen news' for me. I vowed that I would not worry about him based just on rumours from the likes of Peedy Wilson or George Roamers.

By the end of the first week of school, I was feeling a heck of a lot better than I had a year earlier when Billy was still in the neighbourhood. Add to that, something that happened right out of the blue. I had fallen madly, hopelessly in love again. My amorous feelings, though emanating from the heart of a twelve-year-old, were filled with desire for no other person than the woman who welcomed us into our second floor classroom the Tuesday after Labour Day. Miss Garland of Grade Seven, with her luscious red lipstick and her dark hair cut stylishly short, was at least thirty-five or forty years younger than the grandmotherly Mrs. Goode of Grade Six. (Wilson's estimate) So enamoured was I, that by the time the first weekend of September arrived, I realized that I had not given Billy even a single thought in well over a week.

Still, I was caught off guard by what happened near the end of the first week of school. A sunny afternoon got even sunnier when I saw Mary on Kingston Road as I was coming out of Mr. O'Brien's. Though I hadn't seen her since that Sunday afternoon in the park, she would pop into mind every so often, usually when I was gazing at Miss Garland. "Lolly," she beamed. "I have good news. I'm being sent to your school instead of the other one!"

"You mean you'll be coming to Midland?"

"Yes! The other one seems so far away. And at Midland, I'll know at least one person."

"Who?"

"Why you, silly Billy," she giggled.

"Oh, yeah, right." I wondered if she had any toffee with her.

Without saying much, we walked down the street together then crossed towards the lane. "Oh, let's go down this way," she said, "it looks interesting."

"Okay, sure. Where were you coming from just now?" A casual question, showing interest in everyday village life. A very English thing, I figured.

"Why do you want to know?" We stopped near the fallen log.

"No reason. My grandmother lives down that way." I pointed to the far end of the lane.

"Can we stop here a moment? I have to go back to meet my father in half an hour." She perched on the log. "But I'd like to talk a bit about, uh… that rather personal thing."

"Here, sitting on this log?" I didn't think that was such a great idea. I mean, even after a year you could still see the spot that Billy had gouged out with his blood stained knife. Then I looked at her and remembered my near meltdown in church. The sound of her voice, telling me everything was all right. The kiss in the park. The sweetness of her toffee-tasting lips. "Yeah, this would be a good place to sit."

"Well," she began. "I've just been to see Dr. Logan. Do you know him?"

"I sure do. He helped me and a kid I used to know one day, last year."

"He's a lovely man. My father is still there chatting with him." She plucked a lacy white wildflower from beside the log. "One of the things he told me was that it's best not to make my fainting a secret. I ought to tell one or two friends about it." Here she paused as a couple of younger kids on their bicycles tore into the lane.

"Smoochies, smoochies!" they laughed as they rode past us, splashing through every puddle they could see.

I blushed, and Mary laughed. "I have a brother just like those two."

"He likes kissing?"

"No," she laughed even harder. "He rides his bicycle through anything and everything. Once, back in Reading, he rode it on a newly-paved road and came home covered in oily black tar!"

Black tar. The white flower in Mary's hand. How much more urging did I need? Sitting right where Billy and I were last year, the day he told me about the weird stuff that was happening. It was time to tell a friend everything I knew about Billy and how much I worried about ever seeing him again.

"Oh, Lolly," she said when I'd finished the whole story. "That must be terrible. For both of you."

"Yeah. I hope he never comes back here."

"I suppose I would feel the same way." She twirled the flower between her fingers. "But I wonder how *he* feels."

"Huh?"

"Billy. Do you ever wonder what it must be like for him?"

"I did feel sorry for him a couple of times. But now I just don't even want to know anything about him." I pulled a few baseball cards out of my pocket. *These* were the guys I wanted to know about.

"Lolly," Mary said, "if he does come back, you ought to try to talk to him."

"Why would I do that?" I kept staring at Ralph Branca, a pitcher for the Brooklyn Dodgers.

"You told me he was your friend, and good friends don't turn their backs on others."

"But he's so crazy! He might…"

"You don't want to be outside always worrying about whether he might come after you, do you?"

I looked back up towards the highway where Billy and I had first met, started our friendship, and where later on, he had threatened me on that blustery night in November.

"I guess you're right. But for now, he's still somewhere else. In the west end, I think."

"Friends," she said, handing me the flower.

"Yeah." I took a deep breath. "Good friends, I hope."

"Yes," she smiled. "Definitely."

CHAPTER 28
TELEVISION

The rain was off and on all day Saturday, which meant staying inside even after supper. There would be only a few more twilight games of 'first and home' before the days got too short. Tommy, Willie, and I were down in our rec room, looking at baseball cards and the *Popular Mechanics* magazine Willie had picked up after school on Friday. "Fifty-two's are coming out soon," he said, sitting at the far end of the dusty chesterfield. "Cadillac Fleetwood still costs the most."

"How much?" Tommy asked.

"Around four thousand, five hundred. With automatic transmission."

"My dad says the automatics always break down." Tommy was sitting cross-legged on a section of recently tiled floor. Spread out in front of him was an impressive array of baseball cards; Tigers, Dodgers, and Phillies were his most treasured. "Besides, he likes shifting gears," he continued. "How about you, Rich? When are you gettin' rid o' that old junker your dad drives?"

"Soon, I hope. You got this guy, Tommy?" I handed him Ralph Branca.

"Yeah, I got most all the Dodgers, but not Jackie Robinson. Lemme know if you ever get him."

"I gotta go," Willie said as he picked up the four comic books he was borrowing from me: two *Classics Illustrated*, a *Batman*, and a *Blackhawk*. "Goin' up to Wilcox early tomorrow."

"Hey, *Gang Busters* is on tonight," Tommy said, "I better hit the road too. Oh yeah, that reminds me. I saw that Billy kid today in the barbershop." What?! This was the eyewitness report I was hoping would never surface.

"Oh." My heart sank as I remembered what Mary had said just a day or two ago. Clunk! I just wasn't expecting Billy back so soon.

"He's the kid who tried to burn down your garage, right?" Willie asked.

"Yeah, right." I tried to look unconcerned while shuffling through my stack of big-league players.

As Tommy gathered his cards, he picked one out and tossed it to me. "I got three o' this guy. No charge, Rich."

I looked at the name, Bobby Thomson. At that moment I didn't even want to think about baseball as we climbed the basements stairs, but Tommy filled me in on Thomson anyway. "Real good hitter. Plays for the Giants, same as your Willie Mays." (I'd cut out the photo of the Giants' rookie and scotch-taped it to our bedroom wall.) "But they won't beat the Dodgers for the pennant!" Tommy went out the back door and took off up the street. Willie lingered for a minute.

"I was thinking about that Billy kid," he said.

Unsure whether I wanted to talk about him right then, the best I could do was, "Huh? Why?"

"You told me you thought he was crazy."

"Yeah, well..." All I wanted to do was go turn on the radio, flop on my bed, and not think about that kid anymore.

"Why don't you talk to his mom or someone?" Willie suggested, sounding like someone twice his age.

"Geez, Willie..."

"Why not? Maybe she won't like you, but what is she gonna do to you? Shoot y'?" Willie grinned. I laughed a bit too.

"Maybe it would be okay," I said hesitantly, "but you weren't there in the lane that day when Billy went nuts, screaming his head off."

"Maybe he's a lot better now. Anyways, his mom and dad aren't gonna let him do anything crazy."

"I just don't think it's such a good idea, so soon I mean. Not right now." Outside the rain had stopped, and few of the clouds had parted, giving what would be, for most people, a nice view of the setting sun.

"Okay," Willie said, standing on the back steps. "I'll bring your *Blackhawk* and *Batman* to school on Monday."

"Yeah, sure." I went back inside.

"Laurence," Mom called out as I closed the back door. "I have to run down to the church for a bit. John shouldn't be too late getting home," she said stuffing some spools of thread and a bundle of cloth into her Eaton's shopping bag.

"Okay. Where's Nan and Liz?"

"At the Birchcliff. With Patsy and Donna, I think. Oh, and make sure to dust off your pants before you go into your bedroom."

Alone now, I had to think hard about what to do. The radio was no help at all. Just cowboy and quiz shows. I looked at my Jesus picture. The lantern he held seemed to burn a little brighter. Or was it just my imagination? And his hand, as always, was poised to knock at the door. I looked at Bobby Thomson. A great hitter. *What about that pitcher for the Dodgers? Branca? How good is he? What would you guys do if you were me?... Okay, okay. But I'm takin' you two with me... And Rizzuto. Okay fellas, let's go!*

A few minutes later, I was standing inside the front hallway of a house very much like Graddi's. I had knocked on the door twice, but no one answered. As I turned to leave, the door, which was not shut tight, swung open.

I peeked into the living room. There at last, I saw Billy's much talked about television set. It was on, but there was no one in the room watching it. I was so transfixed by the clarity of the images on the TV screen, that for a moment I forgot where I was and why I was there. A woman with blonde, curly-hair was talking on the phone. Golly, she was wearing more lipstick than Betty Grable and Ava Gardner put together!

Oh, don't be such a fraidy-cat, Ethel. It'll be fun!

From behind me, I heard the toilet flush, and again, the sound of a woman's voice. "Who let you in?" Mrs. Northcott came into the living room carrying a glass in one hand and a cigarette in the other.

"Uh, no one, Mrs. Northcott. The door just sort of opened by itself." Polite, but more importantly, proof of my innocence of any attempt to break-in.

"Well, you should have knocked. Anyway, Billy's gone to bed."

"I *did* knock."

Larry Ricciardelli

"Shush, I'm watching the show!" A small woman to be somebody's mother, I thought. She seemed to fit quite nicely into one end of the chesterfield, where she immediately turned her attention to the high jinks on the TV screen.

> We're going to paint this apartment from top to bottom, Ethel. And with this spray gun, we'll have it finished before Ricky even gets home.

Mrs. Northcott let out the first in a series of gurgly laughs at the sight of two women putting on baggy coveralls and hiding their faces behind, what looked like, wartime gas masks. Her cigarette and her drink seemed to add a great deal of pleasure to her television watching. She was laughing so hard that she couldn't stop coughing.

> What are you two doing, dressed up like a coupla Kamikaze pilots?

A short, balding man entered the scene and stood with his hands on his hips. He appeared to have a natural scowl etched into his already craggy facial features.

> If you think I'm gonna help you two scatter brains mess this place up with that spray gun, you got another thing comin', ladies. You can count me out!

At that moment I wanted to be counted out too. I hadn't planned on being all alone with Billy's mom. I was on the verge of saying I was sorry to have interrupted when Billy walked into the living room. Wearing just his underpants and a white T-shirt, he stood at the edge of the carpet, arms folded. So this was it. As often as I had imagined this meeting and how terrifying it might be, I found myself once again mesmerized by his presence.

"Billy, go back to bed! You know what the doctor told you." Mrs. Northcott turned awkwardly as she leaned forward spilling her drink on the carpet. "Now, look what you've made me do!"

"Maybe I should go," I cut in. I didn't want to be around to see Mrs. Northcott punish Billy.

She'll whip me! I know she will. His words echoed inside my head.

Radio Kid

"No, please don't go." Billy sounded friendly enough, something I was not expecting at all. But his mother? Holy Smoke!

"Always having to clean up your mess!" she barked as she pulled herself up and wobbled out into the kitchen. "Now, back to bed!"

Billy rolled his eyes. "Pay no attention to the woman in the alcoholic stupor," he said. "Come on and enjoy the show."

I was just beginning to feel a little bit comfortable with Billy when Mrs. Northcott yelled from the kitchen, "I heard that. Just wait 'til your father gets home!"

"Oh, this is a wonderful show," Billy said, plopping down on the chesterfield. "Come. Sit." He patted the cushion next to him. On the screen, the two women were making a mess of the apartment with the spray gun. The audience was howling.

I wanted to say okay to Billy, but instead, I mumbled, "Gee, I don't think it's such a good idea… I mean, your mom sounds pretty upset." I perched on the arm at the far end of the chesterfield. I'd show Billy a few of my cards, like a regular kid. Then his mom might not be so upset. I pulled the top two out of my shirt pocket.

"Oh, I'm more than upset." Mrs. Northcott returned with a wet dishrag in one hand and a bottle of whiskey or whatever it was she was drinking in the other. "You," she said, looking directly at me, "are the supposed friend who's caused my son so much trouble."

"Mother, would you please stop!" Billy grabbed the dishrag from her hand. "I'll clean the spot on your precious carpet."

Mrs. Northcott remained on her feet as she refilled her glass with a surprisingly steady hand, spilling not a single drop of the precious light brown liquid. "So, Lorrie or Lonnie or whatever your name is, how about telling us what you really told the police? You blamed him!" She pointed at Billy with her cigarette hand. "You told them it was my son who tried to burn down your gar… garbage." Her words melted into a slur. "I mean your gar… garage." She turned awkwardly back towards the TV screen.

"Oh, Mother, you can't even talk straight." Billy shook his head.

"Quiet! I'm trying to watch my show." How could she be so angry and watch a show where the audience was laughing so uproariously? I was afraid to say anything about the fire and the police, figuring she would just get angrier and louder.

A sharply-dressed, dark-haired man came on the screen.

> Lucy? You got some 'splainin' to do.
> Now, Rickey, don't get mad. Ethel and I can fix everything.
> Uh, I gotta go get Fred's supper.
> Madre mia!

Mrs. Northcott raised her glass in the direction of the dark-haired man. "Where do they get these people like Rickey Ricardo there? Talks like a damn D.P.! Another foreigner, just like *his* father." She nodded towards me without taking her eyes off the screen. I didn't know what to do. Just stay quiet and pretend to be polite?

Before I could utter a word, Billy stood up. "His father is not a displaced person!"

"So, he's just a plain dirty wop then." She spewed a stream of smoke towards the ceiling. "They come over here. Don't know how to speak proper. But they know how to lie all right!" A coughing spasm finally pushed her down onto the chesterfield. "Even to the police," she wheezed.

I swallowed hard. "I don't know what a displaced person is, but I do know that my dad is not a liar! The police figured it out for themselves, Mrs. Northcott." She seemed not to hear me. Instead, she turned her attention back towards the television to the man who talked like a D.P.

Billy walked over and blocked the TV screen. "He's right, Mother. The police knew it was me."

I flashed back to what the police detective had said that day almost a year ago. About having 'a little visit with the young man in Miss Bernie's class.'

Mrs. Northcott shook her head but remained seated. "And now *you're* lying, Billy! Can't anyone tell the truth around here?" She was still angry but didn't seem as drunk now. She leaned forward, put her glass on the coffee table, and took another cigarette from the red-coloured pack. "Truth be damned," she shrugged, striking a little cardboard match. "You go right ahead and believe whatever you want."

"The truth that you got drunk after the police brought me home that day and then you whipped me so hard I could hardly walk?"

"That's enough, Billy! You know the doctor said you're not to get yourself worked up."

This was much more than I had bargained for. "I think I'll go home now."

"You know where the door is. So, go on home. Where you belong!"

"That's always your answer, isn't it, Mother?" Billy threw the dishrag down on the carpet. "You just tell people to leave, to go back to where they came from."

"I really have to go now."

"If you had listened to me in the first place, Billy, none of this would ever have happened. I told you he and his kind were no good. They killed your uncle! In case you've forgotten."

"It was WAR!" Billy shrieked, "A lot of people got killed in the war." Billy suddenly turned and fixed his eyes on the TV screen, and in doing so, he appeared to obliterate not only the sound but also the picture. A light in the front hallway blinked once and went dark. Staggering slightly, Billy collapsed to the floor, his head narrowly missing the coffee table.

In the shadowy twilight, his mother cried out, "Oh, my God!" Then the scene that had so often plagued my imagination—the dreaded moment I'd pictured so many times but had never witnessed—began to play itself out in front of me. I'd seen Billy freeze up, even fall down screaming, but what I was watching now was beyond frightening. My heart raced as I watched Billy begin to throw himself about on the carpet like some sort of hairless wolf man, grinding his teeth and howling out the pain of some deep inner rage. I wanted to run from the craziness, from the uncontrolled convulsion of arms and legs, and from this strange sickness that I was sure would contaminate me. But I stood there as if my shoes were nailed to the floor.

"The coffee table. Don't let him bang his head! He might choke to death!" Mrs. Northcott grabbed Billy's head, which was jerking so violently from side to side I thought his neck would break. "Cushion!" she yelled. "Get a cushion!" The words bounced off me like bullets hitting a Sherman tank.

The next thing I knew, a young woman had entered the room. She immediately pushed the coffee table a safe distance away from Billy's head. "Mrs. Northcott, please let me handle this!" She turned him over on one side. "It's all right," she said calmly as Billy's spastic movements gradually subsided. She carefully placed the cushion next to his head.

Larry Ricciardelli

Mrs. Northcott relaxed just enough to light yet another cigarette. She then collapsed back into her spot on the couch and sat staring at the television set, which had miraculously come back to life. The sound of laughter from the screen seemed to signal an end to the crisis. But I kept on looking at Billy. The steely numbness that had formed a protective barrier around me began to melt away. It was supplanted by an indescribable sense of relief, much like the one I had felt after nearly passing out in church. Billy now lay peacefully on the floor, his eyes closed as if in a deep sleep, for he had won a battle and had silenced some sort of demon raging deep inside him.

"He's fine now," the woman said as she wiped the spittle from around Billy's mouth with a Kleenex.

"Fine? Fine? What's that supposed to mean? He hasn't had this bad a session since the wintertime." Mrs. Northcott poured herself another drink. "And I thought you were going to be here at seven!"

"I'm sorry, Mrs. Northcott. There was an emergency."

"And what do you call this?" Mrs. Northcott continued ranting, but I could not understand why. I felt that she should have been thankful that Billy was all right.

"Now, Mrs. Northcott, you know Dr. Kimble said that you weren't to expect miracles with these new drugs."

"It's a miracle he's still alive after what just happened!"

Billy blinked a couple of times, then stretching his arms, he rolled slowly off the cushion. "Oh," he groaned, rubbing his eyes, "is that you, Miss Gerard?" The woman smiled and nodded. "What happened?" Billy shook his head and pulled himself to a sitting position, leaning an elbow on the coffee table.

"Nothing too serious," said the woman, "now let's have a look at you."

I wondered how he must be feeling. He certainly didn't appear frightened or even upset. It's bad for a few minutes, I told myself, but then it's over. A scary scene in a movie doesn't last forever. Miss Gerard looked over at me as I got up to leave.

"I'd like you to stay for just a minute if you could," she said.

Mrs. Northcott continued to be her normal snarly self. "Stay a minute? What for? Go home! You've seen enough!" Coughing and wheezing, she rammed her half-smoked cigarette into an ashtray that was already overflowing with butts and then left the room mumbling something about "another pack in the bedroom."

Billy sighed as he stretched out on the chesterfield. "Don't mind my mother," he said, staring up at the ceiling. Then with a shiver, he wrapped both arms around himself as if huddling against a sudden cold draft. "Oh, I feel so tired," he yawned.

I was about to say, "But you just woke up," when Billy closed his eyes and in seconds was fast asleep.

"You must be a friend of Billy's," Miss Gerard said as she took a small notepad from her purse.

"Uh, yes ma'am, I was. I mean, I am."

"Well, it's important that you understand what you saw here tonight. I can't go into all the details now, but you should know that a seizure like this one, which appears quite frightening at the time, can also be dangerous. However, in Billy's case, it is relatively rare and occurs only under certain conditions."

"Does watching television make you go like that?"

Miss Gerard smiled. "I think that's pretty well been ruled out by now. But we do know that bright flashing lights may trigger a seizure." I wanted to ask if just anyone could catch whatever it was that caused seizures, but Miss Gerard went right on. "And you must understand that all seizures are not as bad as the one Billy had tonight. Many people have seizures that go completely unnoticed."

"But how come the television and the light went off when Billy... uh, started...? I mean, did he make that happen?"

"No, just a coincidence. Brief power outage."

For the first time since knowing of Billy's affliction, I felt unafraid of both Billy and his strange illness. In fact, I wanted to know more. What about Billy's mom? Did Miss Gerard know about the beatings? But this was not the time to ask about that. I could hear Mrs. Northcott grumbling in the back hallway, unable to find her cigarettes. I took a last look at the television. A man in a suit appeared on the screen:

> Brought to you each week at this time by Reingold
> Brothers, makers of fine tobacco products since 1851.

"Miss Gerard," I said, "could I talk to you some other time about, well... um, the thing that Billy has?"

"Well, I'm afraid I'm not permitted to talk about Billy specifically, but we could have a talk about the condition in general. Do you understand what I mean?"

"I think so."

"Would you ask your mother to call me?" Miss Gerard handed me a small card as she saw me to the front door.

"So, Billy isn't really, um... crazy, is he?"

"No more than you or I," she assured me. That confirmation coming from someone who knew what she was talking about was the best thing I could have asked for. "All is well," she added, flicking on the outside light. I wished I could have stayed and talked to her a while longer, but I figured Mom would be wondering where on earth I was.

"Where in Heaven's name have you been?" Mom hung up the phone as I walked in the door.

"I think we should sit down first," I said. After all, I didn't want either one of us passing out as I went over the details of what had just taken place in a house less than a block away.

"Are you sure you're all right, dear?" Mom asked when I'd finished my story.

"I think so," I said, despite feeling a little shaky.

"Well, thank goodness it's over now," she sighed. "It did sound terribly frightening. How about a nice cup of tea?"

"That sounds good. And maybe some chocolate cookies?"

"Anything else while we're at it?"

CHAPTER 29
THE MOST BEAUTIFUL TIME OF THE YEAR

Mr. Welby lived on Sandown, the first house up from the corner. He waved at me from across the street as I stood watching him methodically rake the leaves from his lawn out to the edge of the road. When the pile was to his liking, he struck a match, first lighting his pipe and then setting fire to the leaves. Almost magically, with every puff of his pipe, the flames seemed to spread across the small mound of brown and golden remnants of summer. Mr. Welby tended his fire in an unhurried way, adding just enough leaves to the pile to keep the flames gently dancing. Sweet-smelling smoke spiralled up into the air, marking the advent of crisp, chilly days to come, not to mention the start of the hockey season and the World Series.

I got home from Mary's place on that glorious Thursday afternoon just in time to see Dad pulling out of the driveway. From our front gate I yelled, "Hey Dad!" He looked at me and grinned. That's all I needed, just an acknowledgement that we were on good terms.

Up the stairs and in the back door, I yelled, "Mom, guess what?"

"You got a hundred on an Arithmetic test?" She looked at me briefly, then plopped two handfuls of potatoes into the kitchen sink.

"Better than that. Mary went out and bought some baseball cards just so she could replace the Mickey Mantle one she scrunched up."

"Well isn't that nice of her,"

"Yeah…indeed! And even more amazing she got two!"

"Two what?" Mom began peeling the spuds.

"Two Mickeys! She's keeping one for herself because she thinks he looks like me."

"Wonderful, dear. Now aren't you glad you joined the choir?"

"Oh yes," I sighed. "I'm still on cloud nine." I plunked down on a kitchen chair. "One more thing, Mom. You know that guy Bobby Thomson, plays for the Giants? Well, he hit a homer in the last inning, and they beat the Dodgers. In a playoff game yesterday!"

"Well, that's wonderful, dear. I'm sure a lot of people are very happy about that," she said, rinsing her hands and drying them on her apron. "I'll leave those for the girls," she added, coming over to sit down at the table.

"It sure is wonderful! And get this. He's the guy that Tommy gave me for free. Just before I went over to Billy's house that night. Remember?"

"I certainly remember your going to Billy's house, but I don't honestly remember this 'guy,' as you call him. And what does that have to do with his getting the winning goal for his team?" (I had been meaning to bring Mom up-to-date on baseball parlance, but that would come later.)

"It was good luck, Mom. Don't y' see?" I pulled right up to the table as Mom poured herself some tea. "Tommy gives me a player he doesn't want, a guy who becomes a big-time hero, I go to Billy's house with him in my pocket, and things turn out all right... I mean, it's not so scary anymore." I didn't mention that Thomson's team, the New York Giants, was now in the World Series against another New York team, the Yankees. That would be just too hard to explain without Tommy alongside to help me out.

Mom sipped and smiled. "Well, my dear, if that's what you want to think, then good for you. Just don't go and spend all your money on baseball cards for good luck."

"Okay, but you know what else? Something not so wonderful?"

"But not tragic, I hope." Mom could tell I wasn't exactly heartbroken.

"I lost him and another guy somewhere. I've looked all over." *Losing a player like Thomson* could *mean bad luck, not just for his team but for me too.* But I kept that thought to myself.

"I'm sure they'll turn up. Would you like to get the milk out of the fridge and set the table? Fork goes on the left," Mom reminded me just before Nan and Liz walked in the door.

"Le pain, maman." My oldest sister dropped two brown paper-wrapped loaves of bread on the counter.

"I could eat a *whole* loaf myself," said Liz, plunking down at the table. "I am famished!"

"In that case, my dear, you can start chopping some onions to go with the round steak mince. And Nanette, would you finish up les pommes de terre s'il vous plait?

"Mais oui, avec plaisir."

'Au menu ce soir,' as my Grade Eleven sister would say: mashed potatoes, ground beef with peas and onions, topped off with thick slices of bakery-fresh, heavily buttered white bread. Could you get much farther removed from la cuisine francaise? Both my brother and I added flavour to this solid but not so savoury dish by smothering it with ketchup.

"So who y' rootin' for in the series?" John said as we sat down to supper.

"I don't know yet. I really like that guy Thomson, but Mickey Mantle is on the Yankees. He was the very first baseball card I ever got."

"I heard the Giants won the first game today. In the Yankees' ballpark," my brother remarked, pushing back from the table.

"I know. That's what some big guy in Mr. O'Brien's store was talking about," I said, stretching for the ketchup.

"Well, I hope you are all aware that Princess Elizabeth and the Duke of Edinburgh are coming to Toronto next week," Mom said as she moved the ketchup bottle out of reach. "Enough is enough, Laurence."

"And just think," said Nan, "she'll be queen one day. And she's completely fluent in French. Saviez-vous que?"

"Huh? I mean, pardon me?" Out of the corner of my eye, I noticed Mom grinning.

"It means, mon petit, 'Did you know that?' And did you know that your young Mickey will one day be *the* centre fielder for the New York Yankees?"

"Really?" I had no idea Nan knew that much about baseball.

"Uh-huh. That same very nice boy in our Math class told me."

"That Weller guy you told me about?" Liz said.

"Actually, his name is Wells. Brian Wells. Doesn't that have a nice ring to it?"

"Did he say anything else?" I was always on the lookout for something I could dazzle Tommy and Peedy with.

"Something about Mickey Mantle taking over from a very famous player, I think."

"Joe DiMaggio," John interjected. "According to Stan, he's retiring after this season."

"Really?"

"Stan knows his baseball." That was my brother's exit line, and as was his custom, he pilfered a fork's worth of mashed potatoes from my plate as he got up from the table. He then immediately headed for the back door.

"What's your hurry, John?" Mom asked.

"Someone just got back into town."

"Quel-qu'une from Meaford?" Nan said.

"How'd y' guess? And she is *spectacular*!"

Nan's bilingual brilliance gave her le dernier mot. "Ah, c'est tres magnifique!" she said as my brother skipped out the back door grinning from ear to ear.

A little later, I sat dunking a piece of bread into my heavily sugared cup of tea while Nan and Liz were doing the supper dishes singing a hit song from the Tops In Pops chart. "Girls," Mom said as she got up to answer the phone, "not quite so loud, please." At the same time, there was a knock at the front door. "See who it is, Laurence," Mom said, holding the phone to her chest. Not too often someone comes to the front door, I thought as I walked out to the front hall and flicked on the outside light. With the door open just a crack, I looked out.

"Is your mother home?" Mrs. Northcott asked.

I opened my mouth, but no words came out. "It's all right," she broke the silence. "I've just come over to apologize." She spoke softly with a bit of a smile.

Finally I spoke. "She's on the phone, but…"

An awkward minute or so of silence passed before Mom got to the front hall. "Mrs. Northcott, please come in." She reached around me and opened the door the rest of the way.

"I can only stay a minute," she said, "but thank you."

We sat in the living room. Mrs. Northcott explained that she wanted me there to hear what she had to say. "A few weeks ago, the night you came over to our house, I was in a very bad state." She paused to offer Mom a cigarette before lighting her own. "You're fortunate not to be a smoker. I've tried to give it up so often, but…" her voice trailed off. "What I want to say is that I'm sorry for acting so rudely, especially for saying those things about Mr. Rick-er-delly." (Neither Mom nor I said anything about her mispronunciation.) "I hope you can understand what a terrible year it's been with Billy," she went on.

"Yes, I can imagine. Laurence has told me about some of the problems Billy's been having. Will he be coming back to school?" That was the question I wanted to ask, but I felt I should just sit and listen. Meanwhile, Mom poured two cups of tea. I would get mine later.

"Not for quite a while," Mrs. Northcott sighed. "We're waiting to see how this new medication works out. And, of course, he'll be in the hospital from time to time." She went on to tell Mom about Miss Gerard and Dr. Kimble. "It's more than medication that Billy will need. He's really very lonely. Sometimes I think he spends too much time watching the television set. But then again, that's all he has. He's read everything we have in the house." She paused to light a second cigarette. "I'm so glad he likes to read as much as he does. He gets that from my sister, and Billy does love to spend time at her place out on the Queensway."

"Our teacher, Miss Garland?" I piped up. "She says they're going to have a bookmobile coming around to the school once a week. It's like a library on wheels."

"I hope that means the children will be reading more," said Mom as she offered to refill Mrs. Northcott's cup.

"Oh, no, thank you. I have to leave shortly. An early morning doctor's appointment." She stifled a cough before crushing her partially-smoked cigarette in Dad's big, stand-up ashtray.

"Are you taking Billy to see Dr. Kimble tomorrow?" I asked.

"No. This is with my own doctor. I've been having breathing problems lately." As she got up to leave, she looked at me and said, "Don't ever start smoking, Laurence. It will do you no good."

"Mrs. Northcott, thank you for coming over. I'm sure everything will turn out for the best," Mom said, walking her to the door.

"Oh, I almost forgot. I think Laurence may have left these at our house." She opened her purse and handed me two baseball cards.

"Oh, yeah! Indeed. I looked all over for these guys. I thought they were gone. Thanks a lot."

A while later, Mom and I were back at the kitchen table where I kept glancing at the clock. *Rescue Squad* would be coming on soon. In the meantime, it was 'tea for two and talking time.' The only time I could remember having so many cups of tea was when I wet the bed at Graddi's house when I was in Grade One. "Boy, Mrs. Northcott sounded so different from the night I was at their house."

"Well, I'm sure she is really a very good person who is trying to cope with some very difficult problems, so she drinks and smokes more than she should."

"I kinda felt sorry for her, too. The way I did with Billy sometimes." I dipped the tip of a Chocolate Bourbon cookie into my lukewarm tea. With the soggy, sweet mixture halfway in my mouth, I looked up at the clock. "Time for Hal and Sal," I blurted, jumping up from the table.

"Pardon me?" Mom said.

"*Rescue Squad*! Gotta go."

"Not too late," Mom called out as I dashed to the bedroom, "school tomorrow."

I lay on the bed, half-listening to the 'drama' unfold from inside the little Crosley. Oh, I was still a big fan of the show, but the episode that night was kind of 'mashed potato-ish'; it was about some kid and his dad out fishing and getting their boat caught in the weeds. In other words, not very interesting. In situations like this, I usually leafed through a comic book or snuck a look at John's hockey scrapbook, with the radio on in the background of course. The season would be starting in a week or two, just as the World Series was coming to an end. This would also be a good time to sort out my ever-growing baseball card collection with my two lost players now back in the fold.

I went to the most recent pictures my brother had added after the Maple Leafs' Stanley Cup win. Front and centre on the page was the great photo of Bill Barilko's game-winning goal. I remembered being so tired the night of the final game that I couldn't stay awake to listen to the overtime play by play on the radio. Everybody though, awake or not, knew the result of the game and the name of the guy who had scored the winner. Did they ever call Barilko 'Billy'? I wondered. Then the really sad part of *that* story came back to me: the news that Bill Barilko had been killed in a plane crash just a few months after the Cup victory.

But now I had the young Mickey Mantle and some of his teammates to keep thoughts of baseball alive through the winter. *There's the catcher, Yogi Berra. And his real name is Lawrence. How about that! But just like me, I'll bet almost nobody ever calls him that....And I'm pretty sure that Joe DiMaggio is Italian. Too bad I don't have his card, and I guess I'll never get to see him play now, even if we do go to the New York someday. Same thing for Barilko... Wonder if hockey games will ever be on television? The World Series is on TV... Wonder when we'll ever get a TV? Well, I can always watch it at Christopher's.* As I lay there, scrapbook and cards on my chest, I looked over at my picture of Jesus standing at the cottage door. Still holding the lantern high, He turned to face me. And in that split second glance, He gave his nod of approval.

From the radio:

> Goodnight, kids, and be sure to tune in again next week for another exciting episode of *Rescue Squad*, brought to you by Wheat Strong, the breakfast of patriots. Click.

EPILOGUE

Hockey cards had just come in. It was a couple of days before Halloween, and I was on my way to the smoke shop to meet Willie and Peedy Wilson. When I got to Kingston Road, I just about tripped over a crack in the sidewalk. There was Billy, just stepping out onto the street in front of the barbershop. His slicked-down haircut now sported an up-front, carefully combed wave, an accoutrement my unruly mop would never allow. You could smell the Wildroot Cream-Oil all the way to the corner. That was what Mr. Storey now doused everybody with, like it or not. We stared at each other without saying a word. Other than his haircut, he looked much the same as he did the last time I saw him, the night of his seizure back in September.

"Well, fancy meeting you here, Lolly Pop," he said, striking the pose of an Eaton's catalogue model, his hands in the pockets of a stylish, burgundy-coloured Desi Arnaz jacket. Feeling my face redden as it always did whenever he called me Lolly Pop, I turned and mindlessly began to survey the row of empty Coke bottles inside Mr. Staley's front window. "We could have been close friends, you know."

"Yeah, we could have," I shrugged. A couple of little boys came out of Mr. O'Brien's wearing ghoulish Halloween masks. They would, no doubt, be banging on neighbourhood doors the night after tomorrow yelling, "Trick or treat!"

"Dressing up for Halloween?" Billy grinned.

I wanted to say, 'Yeah, let's go out together.' But I settled for something safer. "Probably goin' to a party at Eddie's place."

"Oh darn, I didn't get an invitation. Boo-hoo … But speaking of Eddie," he said reaching into his pocket, "Here's something of yours I've kept ever since that day I ran into you guys in the lane."

"My pen!"

"A nice little writer." He smiled as he handed it to me. "Miss Gerard said she thought I should hang onto it until the right time came along. So I guess this is that time."

"Geez Billy, I practically forgot about it." Feeling a little choked up I managed a half-hearted, "Why don't you… uh, keep it."

"Thanks, but no thanks, Lolly. Makes me think about a time I'd rather forget. It's your pen anyways"

"Yeah. This was a present from my uncle," I said, gazing at the pen as if I'd just unwrapped it on Christmas Day. Then there was that dreary speechless silence between us tempered only by traffic noise and the smelly growl of a bus pulling out onto the highway. I stood staring into Mr. O'Brien's display window while Billy turned away to look at the bus.

"I'll be moving out to my aunt's tomorrow," he remarked, seeming to trail the view of the bus as it rolled towards the city. When the words sunk in, I thought, why now after all this time? It was funny how disappointed I felt at that moment, whereas a year earlier, I would have rejoiced at the news.

"Oh… uh, you gonna be away for long ?"

"A year, maybe a little more. She lives out near the hospital, you know." Neither of us seemed in a hurry to end whatever was going on between us. I felt like telling him that I wasn't afraid of him anymore, that I truly hoped he would get better, and that I liked that he was different from most everyone I knew.

"What about…?" I said.

"Seizures?" he said with a slight shrug, "I'll probably always have them, but the meds help quite a bit."

"Meds?"

"Doctor talk for medication. Pills, in other words."

BEEP! BEEP! Mr. Northcott's big green sedan pulled over at the corner. (Willie had earlier identified it as an Oldsmobile.) "Well, time to get packing. See you again sometime. Maybe." He gave me one last look with those clear blue Husky dog eyes. "Lolly and Billy," he grinned. Then he climbed into the front seat beside his dad. I waved but he didn't turn around.

As they pulled out onto Kingston Road, Willie and Peedy arrived at the corner. "Was that Northcott?" I could tell Peedy was going to make some jerky comment.

"Yeah. What of it? He's a good friend of mine."

Willie grinned, "Same goes for me."

"What?" Peedy couldn't believe what he'd just heard. "You don't even *know* that nutcase."

"So what?" said Willie. "Lolly knew him, and *he's* a good friend of mine."

"Huh? I don't get it."

"Ask your mother, Peedy. She's a nurse, isn't she?" I laughed.

Mr. O'Brien's doorbell jangled as we walked in.

"Your friend Tommy was in about half an hour ago," he said, picking up the phone. "He almost bought me out of the new hockey cards. I'll have to order another batch."

Peedy and I bought the four packs that Mr. O'Brien had left. Willie went for a *Classics Illustrated* version of "*From the Earth to the Moon.*"

"Hey!" Peedy could hardly contain himself. "I got Rocket Richard and the Montreal goalie, Gerry McNeil."

"Yeah, but can y' beat this?" I countered, holding up a card. "Billy Barilko's winning goal. And there's McNeil with the puck flyin' past him."

"Okay, but Montreal's gonna win the cup this season." Peedy was already into his second pack. "By the way, his name is *Bill* Barilko, not *Billy*," he added.

I chuckled at that one. "I like the sound of Billy better."

Mr. O'Brien hung up the phone. Finally. "I'll have more tomorrow, lads. Better get here before Tommy does."

"Almost five thirty," Willie piped up. "Time for *Sergeant Preston of the Yukon*."

My two friends left the smoke shop in a hurry, Willie with his rocket ship comic book in hand, and Peedy with Maurice 'Rocket' Richard in his pocket. But I took my time, and thought about Billy as I walked past the barbershop where we'd first laid eyes on each other. Back then, it had been Brylcream. Now it was, Wildroot Cream-Oil. Both those brand names had a nice ring to them, just like Hal and Sal or Lolly and Billy.

About the Author

Now retired, Larry Ricciardelli was a teacher at Forest Hill Collegiate in Toronto for thirty-four years. For *Radio Kid* he drew inspiration from his wonderful childhood memories of family, friends, and of course radio shows. The author's love of sports history is showcased well throughout his first novel.

He currently lives with his wife, Mary, and their dog, Piper, in Hastings, Ontario.

CPSIA information can be obtained
at www.ICGtesting.com
Printed in the USA
BVHW072304270223
659274BV00006B/45

9 781039 129542